# PACZKI DAY

## Stories About Growing Up Polish in Detroit

### BOB DOMBROWSKI

PAGE PUBLISHING, INC.
New York, NY

First originally published by Page Publishing, Inc. 2019

ISBN 978-1-64544-062-8 (Paperback)
ISBN 978-1-64544-063-5 (Digital)

Printed in the United States of America

This book is dedicated to my mom, Henrietta Dombrowski; my favorite Polish cook and to my dad, Chester, my sister, Toni and brother, Mike. I hope all four are up in heaven together enjoying a great polish meal.

*To be defeated and not submit, is victory:*
*To be victorious and rest on ones laurels is defeat.*

—Jozef Pilsudski
Poland's Chief of State
1918–1922

*I issue a warning to all those pushers, rip-off artist*
*And muggers, it's time to leave Detroit,*
*Hit Eight-Mile Road!*

—Coleman Young
Mayor of Detroit
1974–1994

*I'd love to be able to say that I came from Detroit.*
*That would be like the coolest thing I could ever say.*

—Anthony Bourdain
1956-2018

# ACKNOWLEDGEMENTS

I WOULD LIKE TO THANK my wife, Linda, for her photography and editing, Chris Smith for his computer savvy and Kamie at Page Publishing for helping me to put it all together. I also want to acknowledge my friends, and relatives and neighbors. Without them, there would be no story.

# PRELUDE

THIS IS MY SECOND BOOK. My first was about my career as a Detroit firefighter. This second book is a mix of stories about growing up in Detroit, going to Catholic school, and the Polish people.

One of the things I learned, as a fireman, was that it takes three things to make a fire: air, fuel, and heat. Remove one, and you can't have a fire. I think it takes three things to make everything. The three things that took to make me and this book: Polish ancestry, the city of Detroit, and the Catholic Church. If you have one or two or maybe all three of these things, you may like this story.

I have tried my best to present everything in this book accurately and most of it is. But I don't have a research staff like the famous writers have. It's just me, my computer, my memory, a big pile of books, and note cards that I painstakingly used to put this story together.

So if your mom wore a babushka, if nostrovia is your toast, if you had a last name that kids made fun of, or you grew up reading your catechism while looking at church steeples and smokestacks, maybe this book is for you.

# Easter with the New Buick.

GOOD FRIDAY WAS ALWAYS A solemn time for Polish Catholics. We didn't eat meat on Good Friday, or any Friday back then, and from noon to 3:00 p.m., the time when Christ died on the cross, we did absolutely nothing. We did not watch TV or listen to the radio or play outside. We just sat around the house with our rosary, or we went to church.

This was Good Friday, 1963, and my mom and I were headed to church in our brand-new Buick LeSabre. I mention the car because nothing was more important to a twelve-year-old Polish Detroit boy back then. Cars were our sports teams. Our fathers all worked for the auto companies. Most of our Irish friends' fathers worked for the city, our Italian friends' fathers poured cement or made pizzas, and the English dads rode the bus downtown where they had office jobs. But our dads, the Polish dads, made the cars. That's what we were here for. They called them the big three. They were Ford, General Motors, and Chrysler. Whichever one your dad worked for, that's the one you loved and cheered for. My dad worked for General Motors.

We only had three cars growing up: a 1949 Chevy, a 1956 Chevy, and then the new Buick, which my mom was now carefully maneuvering to church. We were not going to our local parish, Saint Suzanne's, this Good Friday. We were going to a Polish church where Good Friday's service would be in the traditional Polish way, which was to crawl down the church aisle and kiss Jesus feet. My mom was a great person, but the one thing she wasn't great at was driving. In fact, she was horrible.

Mom grew up in the old neighborhood around Michigan and Central where many people seldom drove. They rode buses or streetcars, or they walked. When we moved out to Orangelawn Street, where houses had big lawns and driveways and everyone drove cars, my dad was determined to teach her to drive. But she never quite got it.

*So far, so good,* I thought when we arrived and mom parked the big Buick in the lot and we headed for the church. We walked in the front door, and the first thing I saw was a line of people down on their knees crawling toward the front altar. My mom got in line and dropped to her knees, and I got behind her. Slowly we crawled down the aisle. As we moved up, people were crawling back past me on my left. We proceeded past each of the Stations of the Cross, carved plaques hanging on the church wall, each one telling another horrible episode of Christ's last days on Earth nearly two thousand years ago.

As I got closer to the altar, I could see they had laid a large crucifix on a low table at the foot of the altar, and when we reached the front of the line, we were supposed to kiss Christ's feet, then turn around and crawl back. As I inched closer, I knew this would be a problem. All these people kissing his feet; all these germs! I can't do it! Then my mom reached the front, bent over, kissed Christ's feet, turned around, and started to crawl back. It was my turn!

I bent over and moved my lips closer, but I couldn't do it; I couldn't kiss those feet. All those people and all that slobber and germs! I just froze right there on my knees. The line was piling up behind me. The folks behind me were starting to grumble. My mom had stopped, turned around, and was giving me one of her looks! "Bobby, what's the matter with you?" she said.

Yes. What's the matter with me? Why can't I kiss those feet? Everybody else is. They don't seem to have a problem. Maybe it's because I'm not supposed to. Maybe it's because I'm some kind of a germ phobic. Or maybe I'm a possessed demon like that one nun said, and Christ is stopping me from kissing his feet, or maybe it's the slobber. Just think of all those cooties!

"Kiss his feet, Bobby!" my mom yelled out, and I did, just that quick! I turned around and started to crawl back behind a very angry mom. I couldn't wipe my mouth because everyone in line was looking at me and would see me. How sacrilegious that would be? We reached the front door, got up on our feet, and walked outside.

"What were you doing there? Why wouldn't you kiss his feet?"

"Mom, those feet had slobber and germs all over. You could get sick from that!"

"Those were Jesus Christ's feet. You can't get sick from them," she screamed!

"Those weren't Jesus's feet. That was a statue made up of plastic," I said.

"Your father and the nuns are right. There is something the matter with you! This is the last time I'm ever bringing you anywhere."

My dad usually never had anything good to say about me. He would say things like, "You're going to grow up to be the next Hitler or the next Al Capone!" Pretty rough stuff for a twelve-year-old. My mom would be standing behind him shaking her head up and down.

So we got in the car and headed home. Mom was still mad, I was just hoping we didn't hit anything on the way home, and thank goodness we didn't.

Saturday. We colored eggs using beet juice for the reds, onion-skins for the browns, and food color for the blues, greens, and yellows. They were beautiful.

Meanwhile, my dad headed to Warren Avenue to pick up a Polish ham and some kielbasa from Mahalaks Meat Market, then down the street to Warrendale Bakery for some Easter egg bread and one of those butters shaped like a lamb. A Polish Easter table wouldn't be complete without one. Dad then brought all this food to the church to be blessed by the priest.

Easter Sunday we woke up to find our baskets. "Who wants to trade their orange jelly beans for my red and green?" I asked my two sisters. "No candy until after church!" Mom yelled from the kitchen.

We never had breakfast on Sunday mornings because we were going to communion. Back then, you had to fast four hours before receiving communion. And this being Easter Sunday, you had to go to communion. If you didn't, that meant you didn't perform your Easter duty, which meant that you could be kicked out of the Catholic Church! Wow. Nobody wanted that.

We got dressed in our Easter finest and loaded into the new Buick with Mom driving. Mrs. McCusker, our next-door neighbor, rode in the front passenger side, and all of us kids piled in the back. My dad had already left for church in the old Chevy. He was an usher and had to be there early.

Mom backed the Buick down the driveway and then headed down West Chicago Road toward Saint Suzanne's. She made a right on Westwood and then another right into the parking lot. The lot was pretty full, but she managed to find an empty parking space along the back fence. Mom then decided to back into the parking space. Why she decided to back into the spot rather than just drive in, I've wondered for years.

As mom slowly backed the new Buick in, I heard a noise from behind and looked back in horror. She had backed over the chain-link fence. Now the fence's top pipe was just an inch or two from the rear window and about to smash through. "Mom, look out!" I yelled. She immediately shifted from reverse to drive and floored the gas pedal.

Whether everyone in front of us in the parking lot jumped out of the way, I don't know, but miraculously, no one was hit as the big Buick lunged forward smashing into cars. Yikes! The first one we hit was a brand-new Chevy Impala, just a week old; I later found out. Then we hit three more cars, four total, before we came to rest. My sister Nancy flew into the front seat and broke her nose. Mrs. McCusker banged her knee, but that was it. The rest of us were okay. A little shaken up but okay. This was before seat belts.

Once the car finally came to a stop, my mom turned back, pointed her finger at me, and screamed, "It's all your fault! If you hadn't shouted, none of this would have happened." Mrs. McCusker also joined in, "Yes. Bobby, it's your fault. You yelling look out caused this whole mess!"

People were starting to run over and open the doors and help us out. Someone got a handkerchief for my sister's bloody nose. All the while, my mother, half hysterical and half sobbing, kept shouting, "It's all your fault! You caused all this!" I didn't say anything. I just stood there watching this crazy scene.

By now, a crowd was forming, and people were starting to look at me. Could it be his fault? Could he be some kind of a little demon who conjured this whole accident up?

There was nothing I could do now, and I was beginning to feel a little uncomfortable. I figured the best thing for me to do was to sneak off and go to church.

I walked in the front door, and the first person I saw was my poor dad.

"Where is your mother?" he asked.

"Well, Dad, I hate to tell you this, but Mom just smashed the car up in the church parking lot."

He just stood there looking at me with that sad, lost look in his face that he must have had so many times in his hard life. He then turned and walked out the door toward the back parking lot.

# Born on Orangelawn

I WAS BORN AND RAISED in Detroit by West Chicago and Evergreen. That's how we said where we lived: West Chicago and Evergreen. We never said Detroit or the West Side just West Chicago and Evergreen or sometimes Plymouth Road and Evergreen. Detroit was huge. There were almost two million people and so we, Detroiters, thought everyone lived in Detroit. When asked, "Where do you live?" we would respond with the two closest busy streets like Woodward and Six Mile, or Vernor and Junction.

My home was on Orangelawn between Patton and Braile, a brand-new brick bungalow my parents moved into on the day I was born. This was 1950, and all the homes in our neighborhood were brand new, purchased mainly by returning GIs from World War II. It was the start of the post-war suburban expansion, although we were still in the city.

All the homes in the neighborhood were smaller bungalows, consisting of a main floor with a kitchen, a living room, a bathroom, and two back bedrooms. The only addition to the main floor was an optional dining room, which we had. Upstairs was an unfinished attic, and downstairs was an unfinished basement. Every home had a front door and a side door but not a backdoor.

This was heaven for my parents and just about every person living in the neighborhood. Many had moved from the old Polish neighborhood down by Michigan and Livernois where they had lived in rented tiny, cold-water flats, which were heated by coal stoves in the kitchen. At least that's what they claimed.

Our house was decorated just like most of my Polish relatives' homes. We had very nice furniture in the living room purchased from J. L. Hudson Department Store and covered in plastic. We were never allowed in there. Our dining room had a classic wood table and matching chairs with a chandelier hanging overhead that we used only three times a year: Christmas, Thanksgiving, and Easter. The rest of the year, we all crammed into the little kitchen; all seven of us (eventually).

My dad fixed up the basement somewhat. He tiled the floor and painted the walls. We threw some old furniture down there and a black-and-white TV and that is where we lived; a true family room. To give the basement a somewhat-exotic look, we covered the exposed light bulbs with paper Chinese lanterns. Also, like all Polish families, we had a second kitchen in the basement, just a stove and a table where my mom could do her big holiday cooking. This was on the other side of the stairs by the washing machine. We didn't have a clothes dryer. Mom hung the clothes in the yard on the clothesline in summer and in the basement in winter. I loved the fresh smell our clothes had.

I slept in the smaller back bedroom with my grandmother until she died. My earliest memory was the priest, Father Roman, coming in to give her last rites. He patted me on my head as he walked by. I was two.

After my grandma died, my new baby sister, Nancy, shared my bedroom. Then a second sister, Toni, was born. The three of us, my two sisters and I, shared a room. Yikes! When my mom got pregnant with my first brother, Ron, my dad was forced to finish off the attic. My two sisters got the big upstairs bedroom at first, then when my second brother, Mike, came along, we switched, and the boys got the big room.

That's how it was at every house in the neighborhood. Everybody had four or five kids, and whoever was the bigger number, boys or girls, would have the upstairs bedroom, and the smaller number crammed into the smaller downstairs bedroom and still only one bathroom.

On the outside, every house had a side driveway going back to the one-car garage. Who would ever need a two-car garage? Next to the garage was the garden. Every Polish home in Detroit had a little garden out back with tomatoes, zucchinis, green peppers, whatever. It is in our blood. So many of us came from a peasant farmer background that we must grow stuff in the summer.

The side drive also filled in for our front porch and back patio. Back in the old neighborhood, the houses and two flats all had big front porches that folks sat out on all summer long. The porches on our bungalows were too small to sit on, and I don't think back decks were invented yet. We would put lawn chairs on the driveway right between the houses and sit and enjoy the summer afternoons and evenings, drinking a cold beer (adults) or lemonade, chitchatting with each other while Ernie Harwell and the Tigers softly blared from our small portable radio. "Kaline's up to bat," My dad said. We all stopped talking and listened to Ernie.

# POLONIA

TO FIND A POLISH NEIGHBORHOOD, you start by looking up toward the sky. When you see the sky filled with church steeples and smokestacks, then look down, and if the streets are filled with tidy little houses with a bar or bakery on every corner, you are there.

The word Polonia means Poland in Latin, which was the language priests said mass in and is often what Polish neighborhoods are called, like Corktown for an Irish neighborhood

The very first Polonia or Polish neighborhood in Detroit was established around the 1860s. It was on the lower East Side by the cross streets of Chene and Canfield. The first Polish immigrants came from the Prussian section of Poland following the Germans who had immigrated earlier. They also followed the German immigrants to church (Catholic, of course).

The first church the newly arrived Polish immigrants attended was St. Mary's, a German-speaking Catholic church on St. Antoine in what is now called Greek Town. Later they went to St. Joseph on Gratiot, also a German-speaking church, but closer to home. As their numbers grew, they soon wanted their own Polish-speaking church.

There were around two hundred Polish families living in this new Polonia. They organized and bought a piece of land on St. Aubin street and built St. Albertus Church which still stands today at 4231 St. Aubin. It is a one-steeple church designed to resemble the churches they left behind in Prussia.

Why they named it St. Albertus, which doesn't sound very Polish is another funny Polish story. They originally wanted to name their new church Wojciecha; very Polish-sounding name. In trying to find a Latin and then Polish equivalent, the name Wojciech somehow turned into Albertus. But whatever the name, they now had their own beautiful church.

This church, St. Albertus, was ground zero for the thousands and thousands of Polish people who immigrated or were born in the Detroit area. The Polish Roman Catholic Union (PRCU), the first Polish News, the Felician Sisters, and the seminary at Orchard Lake St. Mary's all came out of St. Albertus Church on St. Aubin.

As the Polish community grew, they began spreading west across Woodward, down along Michigan Avenue toward Livernois. Soon it became apparent that another church was needed on the West Side. In 1882, the first Polish parish was established on the West Side. It was named Saint Casimir.

They first built a temporary church on Twenty-Third, just south of Myrtle (called Martin Luther King Boulevard now or MLK for short). The temporary church didn't last long. Polish people work fast, and just eight years later, in 1890, they opened a brand-new church at 3401 Twenty-Third Street.

And what a church it was. It was a huge Romanesque Byzantine designed structure that resembled Saint Peter's Basilica in Rome, one of the most beautiful churches in the world!

It was dedicated on December 21, 1890. That morning, all the Polish people met in front of the new church at 8 a.m. They then marched down Twenty-Third, turned left on Michigan Avenue, and marched three miles to Woodward. They stopped at Grand Circus Park where a band was waiting for them and then they all marched to Washington Boulevard to Bishop Foley's residence. Then, along with the bishop, they marched back to the new church and had a huge mass and a daylong ceremony.

This was the neighborhood my parents grew up in. My father went to St. Casimir School. We were West Side Polish. The beautiful church was torn down in 1961 and replaced with a modern, ugly-looking, A-frame church (unbelievable). Nobody seems to know the exact date the new church opened and nobody cares.

When they built the beautiful St. Casimir in 1890, they also built a second identical one in Chicago called St. Mary's of Perpetual

Help. It is still standing and doing well; a proud symbol of the Polish Catholics of Chicago.

Look the church up the next time you're in Chicago, or just Google it. You will wonder, just like me, *who would ever tear down something this beautiful?* A monument from our forefathers! Sure, they gave all the usual excuses. It's too old, it's too expensive to heat, and it's dangerous! But that didn't happen in Chicago, did it?

It was a shame what happened to St. Casimir's, but this was 1961, and people were moving to the suburbs. The old neighborhoods and the old churches didn't look so good in the new modern world. We wanted the split-level homes and the modern A-frame churches out in the burbs. People couldn't tear down all the old homes and replace them with modern ones, but they could tear down the old church and replace it with a modern one, just like the ones being thrown up all over suburbia.

It wasn't just on Twenty-Third Street that this was happening but all over Detroit. Instead of being proud of our old stuff, we wanted to get rid of it and be modern just like the new suburbs. We got rid of our streetcars, our old stores, our old churches, and our old neighborhoods including Polonia. To help, we built modern expressways right through them.

My dad would often take me back to his old neighborhood on Twenty-Third Street. I was upset when they tore down the old church and built the new one. He wasn't. He believed in progress and cheered all the new changes, including the new church. To him, the old European styles meant the old days and the old country and oppression and suffering. The new modern styles represented America and the future with freedom and happiness.

Saint Albertus is still around and has mass only on certain occasions. St. Casimir's closed in 1989; one of ninety-two Catholic parishes that have closed in Detroit.

# THE FIRST AMERICAN POLONIA

DETROIT WAS NOT THE FIRST settlement of Polish Americans, nor was Chicago. The very first settlement of Polish Americans was in Texas, of all places. Panna Maria, Texas, a little town in southern Texas was the home to the very first Polish settlement back in 1854. The name Panna Maria means Virgin Mary.

A Polish priest named Father Moczygemba, who was preaching to the German immigrants living in the area, decided he would invite his people, the Polish, to immigrate there. The exact number who came is not known, but it is guessed to be around a few hundred. They got there after a three-month journey on Christmas Eve 1854, and held Christmas Eve mass under a big oak tree that is still standing today. They started the first Polish American Catholic Church naming it Immaculate Conception. By 1858, there were 120 Polish families living in Panna Maria.

They bought land for their farms from a hustler named John Twohig who sold them land valued at $1.50 an acre for $6.00 an acre. They planted cotton and other crops. Life was hard. They faced floods, droughts, snakes, malaria, grasshoppers, and bands of raiding marauders. It was no American dream. They were so upset that they turned on the person who talked them into coming to America, Father Moczygemba. He took off and moved to Michigan, where he spent the rest of his life.

The local Texans didn't take too kindly to these strange immigrants who didn't speak English. When the Civil War broke out, things got real ugly. Texas was a Confederate State that supported slavery. The Polish of Panna Maria did not believe in slavery and did not support the Confederates. They were terrorized by bands of law-less Texans all during the war and for years afterward.

Railroads never extended a rail line to Panna Maria, so the little town began to shrink. A big bright spot was in 1966 during the Polish Millennium. President Johnson gave them a twelve-thousand-piece mosaic of the Virgin of Czestochowa, the Black Madonna, for their celebrations. A dark spot then came in 1977 when the Chevron Corporation decided to open a nuclear waste dump in the area. After that, nobody wanted to live there. Today less than a hundred people call Panna Maria their home.

# Off to School (Catholic, of Course)

MY LITTLE SECTION OF DETROIT, just like all the neighborhoods back in the 1950s had a ton of kids. When I turned five, I marched with all of them two blocks down to McColl School for kindergarten. It was a beautiful new school with pretty teachers and loads of fun with all the kids from my neighborhood. But it only lasted a year.

The following year was different. I walked one block with my neighborhood friends, then turned left on West Chicago and walked a mile to Saint Suzanne School. It was a big, two-story brick building that looked like a fortress. Inside, instead of the pretty and lively teachers I had at McColl, we had stern-faced nuns dressed in outfits straight out of the middle ages.

The first thing I learned at Saint Suzanne's is there's no screwing around and not much fun like in McColl School. They assigned me a little desk and with the exception of lunch, there I sat for seven long hours, practicing the four R's: reading, riting, religion and rithmatic, in that order.

The highlight of the day would be lunch. I would gobble down the peanut-butter-and-jelly sandwich my mom made for me, wash it down with the carton of chocolate milk I purchased for four cents, then run outside to the parking lot for thirty minutes of pure exhilarating insanity.

We did not have gym class at Saint Suzanne School back then. The gym itself was being used for a temporary church. This was before the actual church was built. So nearly a thousand kids would take all their pent up youthful energy out to the parking lot and accompanying side street (which was blocked off to traffic) and play the only game that we could play on those crowded couple of acres: chase the ball.

Someone would throw a rubber ball into the air, and we would all run after it trying to catch it. When someone caught it, they would throw it back into the air, and the mass would move in that direction. Back and forth we all ran after that ball for thirty whole minutes until the bell rang and in we went for three more hours of the four Rs.

We did have one bit of physical activity. Once a week, Sister would lead us down to the basement for an hour of tap dancing lessons. The basement was the coolest part of the school. A high-ceilinged room about a couple hundred feet long with painted block walls and a brightly colored tile floor; a stage at one end and a kitchen at the other. Nowadays they would probably call it a cafetorium.

The basement we all loved because it was used for all kinds of fun stuff, spaghetti dinners, father-and-son Sunday breakfast, air raid drills (where we would kneel down with our arms over our heads waiting for those godless commies to drop the big one on us), Girl Scouts, Cub Scouts, Boy Scouts (award-winning troop 488), and later Teen Towner's still remembered as the West Side's best teen dances. But our first introduction to the basement was tap dancing lessons.

They would line us up on the tile floor; girls in front, and boys in back. They did this because they knew that boys never knew the dance moves. We would watch the girl's feet in front of us and try to do the same.

"Shuffle step! Shuffle step! Shuffle! Ball change! Shuffle! Ball change!" the teacher would yell out, and we would shuffle along.

Once a year, we would have a tap dance recital at night in the school basement, and our parents would come and watch us dance. The boys would wear white shirts with neckties, and the girls would have fancy dresses. It must have been pretty disappointing for our folks, watching us kids while knowing their tap dancing lesson money was right down the drain.

The cool thing was that we got taps for our shoes. They were metal cleats that my dad would screw onto my shoes on the day of the recital. It would then take him a couple weeks to get around to removing them, so for two whole weeks, my friends and I would walk down the halls, "Tap. Tap. Tap," thinking we were some big greasers at Cody High.

One thing we all learned at Saint Suzanne was Catholicism and how to be a Catholic, such as the seven sacraments: Baptism, Communion, Penance, Confirmation, Marriage, Holy Orders, and Extreme Unction. Penance and Communion were made in the second grade.

Our first Communion was the most exciting day of the second grade. I got all dressed up in my new Communion suit. I got a brand-new little prayer book, a rosary, and something called a scapula—a shoelace with two square pictures of Mary holding baby Jesus. Sister told us that if we wore it around our neck nonstop for the rest of our life, we would automatically go to heaven. Not bad!

On the big day, the whole second grade lined up by height in two long lines: one for girls dressed in their pretty white dresses, and the other one for us boys. I was number seven in the boys' line, not very tall in those days. We then proceeded down the center aisle and passed all our parents and relatives to the altar where Father Lorenze, after saying something in Latin, laid a little round host on our tongue. Receiving that host for the first time was a very big moment in our young lives because we knew that round wafer was actually transformed to the body of Jesus Christ. Then back into our pew to pray without smiling.

Afterward, my parents threw me a big first Communion party, and all my aunts and uncles and cousins came over. Pop, beer, and the best food were served and then topped off with a large communion cake with a little plastic boy on top that I guess was supposed to be me. I kept my new suit on all day and completely ruined it. My aunts and uncles handed me cards with money inside, which I handed over to my parents not to be seen again. All in all, it was a great day.

The second sacrament we made in second grade was Penance, or as we called it confession. Sister taught us that we would go into the confessional, tell the priest our sins, make a sincere Act of Contrition (confessional prayer), and then the priest would forgive all our sins. All our bad stuff would be left behind in that little confessional. We would be brand-new, good, holy people. This would then bring up all the questions every Catholic has.

"Even if someone killed somebody they would be forgiven?" I asked.

"Yes, as long as they were sorry for their sins and made a good confession," sister told us.

"But what if Hitler who killed millions of people went to confession?"

"Hitler wasn't a Catholic. He was an atheist," sister said.

"But what if he became a Catholic and went to confession?"

"Now, children, don't be silly," sister said.

But silly we were, and the questions went on. Sister then told us that if we were about to die and couldn't get to confession, we could just make a good Act of Contrition, and our sins would be forgiven. How great is that? And to this day, me and every Catholic out there, no matter how cynical we have become, when we're in a bad jam, we're saying our prayers; and if we have enough time, we're making an "Act of Contrition," a sincere one!

A daily event that happened at Saint Suzanne and probably every Catholic School in America was the pagan babies. We would collect money every day to be sent to the Catholic missionaries who would go off to places like Africa and French Indochina and convert the pagan babies to Catholics. We all knew that those poor pagan babies who weren't baptized couldn't get into heaven if they died. They could go to limbo if they were good, but limbo's not heaven. So it was with great urgency that our missionaries had to find these kids and baptize them as Catholics before something happened to them.

The morning would start with sister holding up a cardboard milk carton with a slot for coins and asking, "Boys and girls, does anyone have any money for the pagan babies?" And the stampede would start. We would give her whatever money we had: our milk money, our lunch money, communion money, birthday money, whatever. We all wanted to be good Catholics and do our part. I remember a kid gave her five dollars that his grandma gave him for his birthday. Why selfishly spend it on yourself when there are pagan babies to save?

I wasn't as generous as some of my classmates, but I did give what I could. One time I went up there with a dime and asked sister for a nickel change. She looked a little bewildered but handed me my nickel. I needed it for lunch to buy my chocolate milk. After all, a young man must keep up his strength.

# SISTER ELEANOR

FOURTH GRADE IS THE GRADE that I will always painfully remember. A new nun came to Saint Suzanne (probably booted out of some other school) and was assigned to our class. Her name was Sister Eleanor. I still get the chills when I think back about this outrageous nun and what she put us through.

Every Catholic kid has classroom stories of nuns beating the crap out of him back in the day, usually when we stepped out of line. But Sister Eleanor was different. She was the master of agony. No nun ever inflicted pain more skillfully or with more pleasure than our good old, wild and crazy Sister Eleanor.

Sister Eleanor's weapon of choice was a wooden pointer about the length of a yardstick. She would swing this pointer the way an ancient Japanese samurai would swing his sword. Landing every blow with precise accuracy for the maximum amount of pain. It would take very little to set her off, a giggle, a mispronounced word, forgotten homework assignment, whatever, and the wrath of God would be upon us. Sister Eleanor would beat the devil out of us, and I mean that literally.

Here is an example of Sister Eleanor. She caught me talking in class, called me up to the front, and told me to hold out my hands palm side up. She then proceeded to whack my palms with that pointer nonstop until I started to whimper and crying in front of my class as they hid their laughing faces which was the worst part. Sister Eleanor never stopped short of tears. As she was whacking us, hands, legs, arms, rear end, whatever, she would be screaming in tongues! "The devil has possessed you. If you think this is bad, wait till you feel the flames of hell!" And other scary messages straight out of some middle age prayer book.

Usually this would be the highlight of an otherwise boring day, watching our classmates get beat. When it was my turn to get the beating, the only consolation I had was I knew that in an hour or two, it would be one of them, and I would be hiding my snickering face. This was a Catholic tradition in education. Not everyone got a beating, just us screwups. It would keep all the others in line. It was entertainment, and nobody had any empathy for the victims. We were just glad when it wasn't us. Ask any person who went to Catholic school about the nuns hitting the students and watch a smile come to their face. Yes, it was cruel to laugh at our unfortunate classmates getting their beating, but it's what we did.

Fourth grade also meant we would receive our fourth sacrament called Confirmation: the sacrament that would make us solders of Christ. Making our Confirmation required us to do two things: pick a sponsor and pick a Confirmation name. This was the one time in life when you got to pick your own name. And I knew what mine would be right away, Michael for Michael the Archangel.

What could be a more perfect name for confirmation than Michael the Archangel? They taught us that there are three Archangels: Gabriel, Raphael, and Michael. I have no idea what the first two did, but Michael was the one who defended God and heaven back when Lucifer, the angel of light, tried to pull off the first coup in history and take over heaven. Michael, with his sword and shield and armor, defeated Lucifer and the gang of dark angels and sent them all to the depths of hell.

Then we found out that Archbishop Dearden, the head of the Detroit Archdiocese, would be the one confirming us. This put all the nuns in a tizzy but none more than Sister Eleanor. There were a bunch of bishops, but the biggest one was Archbishop John Francis Dearden, soon-to-be Cardinal Deardon, the rock star of bishops. Sister Eleanor warned us in no compassionate terms that we would be on our best behavior and what would happen to us if we weren't. Nobody doubted her.

On the night of Confirmation, the church was packed. The whole family came along with Uncle Hank, my sponsor. They had us walk up to the altar in a procession with our sponsors trailing behind us. We then knelt down, folded our hands, and waited for the bishop. When the bishop got to me, I looked up and gasped. He looked ten feet tall with steel eyes and a big red hat. The giant looked down at me, said some words in Latin along with the name Michael, then slapped the side of my face. It was a moment I'll never forget. I was now a soldier of Christ.

Walking back, Jimmy Shrubbery looked over at me and said, "That slap was nothing compared to Sister Eleanor."

"You got that right," I said and started to laugh. Then I looked up and staring at me with her sternest look was Sister Eleanor. Well, I knew what that look meant. I would be the lead entertainer in class tomorrow.

# THE THREE BROTHERS

ONE CANNOT TELL THE POLISH story without the old story of the three brothers. Many years ago, there was a wandering tribe of Slavic people looking for a land to call home. The old chief had died, and his three sons whose names were Lech, Czech, and Rus now ruled them.

After months of weary travel, the three brothers began to argue over which direction the tribe should go. Lech wanted to go north, Czech wanted to go south, and Rus wanted to go east. They then divided the tribe in three, and each brother took a third of the people and headed in his chosen direction.

Lech and his followers headed north until one day he saw a white eagle majestically flying overhead. Lech knew this eagle was a sign from the gods. The eagle landed in a nest in a large oak tree. Lech climbed the tree as high as he could and looked around. To the north, Lech saw a mighty ocean. To the east, he saw an endless plain of flat fertile land. To the south, he saw hills and mountains. And to the west, he saw a thick, dark forest. Lech climbed down the tree and told his tribe, "We found our home."

They built a town around the tree, and Lech chose the white eagle as their symbol. They named their town Gniezno, which means nest. The town became the first capital of their great nation that they named Lechits after their leader. As time went on, their country became Poland: land of the fields and plains.

The two other brothers Czech and Rus, who headed south and east, also founded countries that still bear their names: Czechoslovakia and Russia.

Most historians believe that the Slavs arrived in Poland in the sixth century, about four hundred years before the arrival of Christianity.

The first Poles were farmers who lived off the land. The word pole means field.

The first Polish were pagans: folks who believed in gods, goddesses, demons, spirits, and all the fun stuff early European societies believed in. But unlike the Greek gods and the Irish leprechauns, most of us Americans know nothing of the old Polish myths. So let me tell some stories!

Mysticism ruled every aspect of the early Polish lives. The earth, the wind, the trees, the rivers, all things, had some sort of spirit, sometimes good, sometimes bad. Their homes, barns, and crops, even their family members could be possessed by the spirits. The Poles spent their entire lives worrying and praying to the gods and spirits. Anything that happened to them was the result of a spirit.

The early Poles were also pantheistic and animistic, meaning they believed everything was alive and held some spirit. Since the earth, the mountains, and the rivers were far older than humanity, their spirits must be wiser. Trees, big rocks, even animals had spirits that could be their ancestor. When you died, your spirit just moved on; no new souls were ever born.

Circles were a big part of the early Polish life. They usually formed circles for worship with a fire or lighted candles. This would protect them from evil. Holidays usually revolved around the equinox and the solstice, which later would be turned into Christian holidays.

Matisyra Zemlia was the most important god. She was the goddess of Mother Earth. When they made an oath, they would hold dirt in their hand as a sacred symbol. When a person was close to death, they would dig a hole and shout into it all their sins. The earth would sometimes shout back, "Give me five Our Fathers and five Hail Marys." I'm joking, of course.

Perun was, I think, the worst god. He was the god of thunder and lightning. The Polish worried that he would ruin their crops with bad storms or no rain. They made July 20 his holiday and what a terrible holiday it was. On that day, they would pick a person to be sacrificed to the god Perun.

The god Jurata was one of my favorites. She took the form of a beautiful mermaid who lived under the Baltic Sea in a palace made from amber. The god Perun fell in love with her, but she didn't love him; she loved a mortal fisherman. Perun, in his rage, threw a bolt of lightning down and smashed her amber palace killing her and her fisherman. To this day, when little pieces of amber wash up on the Baltic shore, it's said to be pieces of Jurata's palace.

Bannik was the bathhouse spirit. Polish bathhouses were actually saunas and were very spiritual places. The fourth bath firing, or the fourth time they used the bathhouse, was always left for Bannik; the spirit and people would stay out.

Djabelek was a troublesome little imp or devil who always caused trouble. To this day, Polish people refer to their kids when they are acting up as Djabeleks.

Vampires, or wampyrs as the Polish called them, are legends in every eastern European country. Poland wampyrs attacked their own family. They would drain their life one by one. After a family member died and another member started getting weak or lifeless, they would believe their dead relative became a wampyr! They would then dig up the body, and if it looked in too good of shape for a corpse, they would chop it up and rearrange the parts, then rebury it.

Domovois was the protector of the house. Usually an old deceased grandfather would come back and become the Domovois. He would try to protect and warn you of future events. If the people heard crying, then bad things would happen, laughing, then good things would happen. People had to be careful with things like what color they painted the house, so as not to offend the Demovois.

Polewiki was a little dwarf with hair made of grass. He would cause much mischief in the fields including getting wanderers lost. He didn't have much use for slackers. If the Polewiki found a field-worker drunk and asleep, he would put a spell on him, and the worker would never wake up.

Zoria was the goddess of beauty.

Swiatowit was a god with four faces who saw in all directions.

Svarog was the god of fire and blacksmiths.

Svetovid was the god of war and fertility.

# THE BAPTISM OF POLAND

THE YEAR 966 IS CONSIDERED the beginning of Poland. It was the year King Mieszko the First was baptized. He made Poland officially a Christian country, outlawing paganism.

This was how it seemed to work throughout medieval Europe. The king would convert to Christianity and would order the rest of the country to follow. The people close to the king would be first to convert, then the townspeople, and lastly would be the country folk who would sometimes hold on to old pagan ways for hundreds of years. They actually had pagan uprisings in 1030. The king quickly put them down, and Christianity became the religion of Poland.

Some pagan traditions merged with Christian traditions. Polish pagans celebrated winter solstice and would bring evergreens into their homes because they thought they held special powers because they stayed green all winter. The Christians switched that to Christmas trees. Pagans celebrated the spring equinox with eggs and rabbits, which symbolized fertility. Those, of course, became Easter eggs and Easter bunnies.

Gniezno was the first capital of Poland and then Poznan. Then in the eleventh century, Cracow became the capital. It wasn't until 1596 that Warsaw (the present-day capital) became Poland's capital.

Poland, because it was a flatland located in the center of Europe with no natural borders, was always under attack from foreign enemies. In 1241, the Mongols from the east began the first of their attacks along with the Tartars who also came from the East. These attacks would go on for hundreds of years.

They would come without warning. There were thousands of them burning, raping, looting, and murdering. The lucky ones would run for their lives to the next town or a castle where they would try to make a stand, usually in vain. Eventually the Polish would get strong enough to hold them off. The Mongols would retreat only to return again. The rewards in Poland were too great to resist.

It's funny that all the looting and victorious battles didn't help the Mongolians very much. They could mount great armies and travel thousands of miles, but they couldn't advance their culture. Poland always got up and rebuilt and advanced until they were too advanced for the primitive Mongolian culture to even consider attacking. As they say, you learn more from a defeat than a victory.

The one thing they did leave behind was a lot of kids. To this day, almost nine hundred years since the Mongol invasions, some Polish people have the high cheekbones and narrower eyes of the invading Mongols of so long ago.

In 1385, Poland and Lithuania were united by the marriage of Queen Hedwig of Poland and Grand Duke Jogaila of Lithuania making Poland one of the largest countries in Europe, stretching from the Baltic to the Black Sea.

As Poland got bigger, it also got stronger, which they needed because of new problems on her western border, Germany, and the Teutonic Knights. The Teutonic Knights were a fierce group of fighters originally organized to protect Jerusalem from the Muslims during the Crusades. Over the years, they fought many battles stopping Muslim invasions into Western Europe. In the twelfth century, the knights returned home to Germany and then started to harass the Polish.

At first, they came as friends to help the Polish fight off and convert pagans in neighboring areas. But soon, the Knights began raiding Polish towns and claiming huge areas of Poland including the whole Baltic coastline for themselves.

But the Polish were not to be messed with. Between them and the Lithuanians, they formed a huge Army and met the Teutonic Knights in what would be the greatest European battle of the Middle Ages in the Battle of Grunwald also called Tannenberg. The battle took place in 1410. Poland won one of her greatest victories and changed the balance of power in Europe for hundreds of years.

During the build up to World War II, Hitler used images of the Teutonic Knights to rile the Germans to fight the Polish. On the other side, the Polish used images of the Teutonic Knights to rile up the Polish to fight the Germans. But ironically, Poland won that battle because today, the castle of the Teutonic Knights or Malbork is located in Poland, not Germany. It is the biggest castle in Europe.

Poland started the first representative or republican government in history. In 1493, each noble sent a representative to Cracow, and they formed a parliament, which they called the Sejm. Then by election, the nobles would choose a king, usually an outsider because they didn't want any noble getting the upper hand. They also adopted a policy called Librium Veto, which meant any noble could veto any proposal with one single vote. The Librium Veto eventually made Poland's parliament (the world's first) useless and ended up destroying their country. The nobles called this system golden freedom. If you had the gold, you were free.

For the next 150 years, Poland enjoyed what they called the golden years. The system seemed to work. They became one of the biggest and strongest countries in Europe. But in the 1600s, it came unraveled. First, the thirty-year war, which left Poland weak and exhausted, then in 1656, Sweden invaded.

The Swedish Army overtook Poland without much of a fight. Then they started raping and pillaging. The Swedes stole everything, and they killed close to 20 percent of the population. They burned monasteries and churches (after looting them). Many historians called this invasion as bad as the Nazis three hundred years later.

Then to make matters worse, our good friends from the east, the Russians, invaded and so did Transylvania and a couple other countries too. Poland needed a miracle, and they finally got one.

In the town of Czestochowa, there is a monastery called "Jasna Gora." It is the home of the famous painting Our Lady of Czestochowa or the Black Madonna. The painting depicts Mary holding baby Jesus, and they are both black. Why they are black is still debated by some, but what's not debated is the miracle that happened there in 1655.

The Swedes attacked the monastery in November. The siege lasted fifty days while a small group of Polish soldiers and monks held off the Swedish Army. The Swedes set the monastery on fire, burning much of the monastery and the famous painting Our Lady of Czestochowa. The painting was burned and darkened but was saved by the Polish monks. They prayed to that painting for a miracle. Then on Christmas day, 1655, the much larger Swedish Army gave up and returned to Sweden.

The monastery today is the third biggest pilgrimage sight in the Christian world. It is a tradition for all Polish young people when they graduate from high school to make a pilgrimage to Czestochowa. The Polish teens come from every town in Poland no matter how far they have to walk.

Go to any Polish house in America and hanging on the wall will be a picture of the Black Madonna. Or you can go to a museum in Sweden and see the rest of the stuff, the art, and treasures that they looted from Poland hundreds of years ago.

# HIDE-AND-GO-SEEK

ONE THING I THINK EVERYONE who grew up in my west side neighborhood back in the fifties and sixties would agree, it was a great place to grow up. Three short blocks from my house was Rouge Park, a three-square-mile playground with the polluted Rouge River running through. We loved it. The crown jewel of Rouge Park was the three Olympic-size pools and a ten-meter diving deck that we just called the pools.

The whole neighborhood would go there every day both periods (a.m. and p.m.). It was our hangout. It was also free. We would walk in the front door of the majestic brick manor; girls go to the left, and boys to the right. We would take a shower and get inspected. While naked, we would have to do a spin around in front of a bored lifeguard, then put our bathing suit on and run off to a freezing pool. They would have the pool's temperature written on a chalkboard: sixty-eight or sixty-nine degrees. On a hot day, it might break into the seventies.

We all learned to swim there thanks to the free swimming lessons. And we learned to jump off the decks, first deck, second deck, and third deck, which was scary. It was thirty-six feet up and once you climbed up, there was only one way down. The lifeguards wouldn't let anyone chicken out and climb down. Once you were up there, you had to jump. We all thought the lifeguards were the coolest dudes in the city. They were college kids with white stuff on their noses, wearing speedos and pith helmets, and swinging their whistles while yelling stuff like, "Slow down and One more time and You're out of here!"

Rouge Park would also be our first encounter with black kids. Our neighborhood was all white. Everyday buses would bring black kids from the inner city to the park. They called it day camp. The a.m. period at the pools would be integrated and the p.m. would be black to mostly white. One day, I was swimming with a black kid, and he told me he had an uncle in Africa who was a cannibal! "Wow! How cool is that?" I said.

Finding those big boxes that washing machines and dryers came in was always a treat. We would drag them to the park, up to suicide hill, then roll down in them pretending they were Army tanks. One day, three of us were having fun rolling down suicide hill when some old pervert exposed himself to us. Jimmy and I didn't pay him much mind but David Green did. He went home and told his mom who went ahead and called the police.

The next day, my mom called me inside and sitting in our living room were two Detroit policewomen. Never in my life have I had an encounter of such importance, and the most important question I had to ask, "Do you carry guns?"

Guns were a huge to us cowboy-loving kids. Nobody had guns back then except for the police. None of my friends' dads owned a gun, and they were all World War II veterans. The only people who had guns were the cops like Chuck Bokowisz's Dad who hid his in a hatbox on the top shelf of his closet. At least that's what Chuck told us.

"Yes, we have guns in our purses," one of the policewomen said.

"Could I look at them?" I asked.

"No, we're not here to show you our guns. We're here to find out what happened yesterday in Rouge Park."

After that, they said we had to go look at mug shots at Detroit Police Headquarters at the infamous 1300 Beaubien. Every boy who grew up on the streets of Detroit knew that 1300 Beaubien was the address of Detroit Police Headquarters. It was just a cool thing to know. Although 90 percent of us would never get a chance to go inside, we all imagined all the cool cop things that went on inside. But now thanks to that pervert we're getting our chance to go see for ourselves.

When we got there, the policewomen took us upstairs on an elevator to look at mug shots of known perverts to see if we could identify our guy. We were shocked to see how many mug shots of perverts there were: hundreds and hundreds. Out of which the three of us positively identified around 150 different mug shots as the wacko we were all looking for. No arrest, but we had a good time.

Mic-Macs was the name of the little league in the park, and everybody played baseball and football for them. When we had a game, everyone would come. They would walk down to the park carrying their lawn chairs. Some parents even bet on the games. I was with my cousin Richard at Frankies Bar on Joy Road where my uncle Ted was a bartender, and some man sitting at the bar asked, "Hey, kid, what team do you play on?"

"The Cardinals," I said.

"A bunch of bums. I lost two bucks on you kids last week."

In the winter, the park had four toboggan runs and a ten-acre ice skating pond. Ice skates were no problem for us even though our feet grew every year. My mom would load us up in the car and drive down to a house by West Chicago and Hubble where for one dollar plus exchanging last year's skates, we got a brand-new pair of sharpened used skates.

Summertime, Aunt Cassie would drive all us kids down to the US rubber plant that she worked at. It was right next to the Belle Isle Bridge. They had a company store where employees could buy US Keds tennis shoes cheap. We would all get a new pair of Keds. That and my Mic-Mac baseball hat was the uniform of summer.

Every night in summer, the whole neighborhood would play hide-and-go-seek. We would have forty or fifty kids running and hiding while parents sat on their driveways drinking a cold Stroh's or Pabst. Goal was the light pole on the corner of Orangelawn and Patton. We would hide everywhere: backyards, bushes, behind trees, and cars, then run full blast to tag goal before getting caught. What a blast! We would play until the streetlight came on, then all go home and go to sleep.

Halloween was the best. Craig's dad worked at the railroad and would line up both sides of Patton with lit railroad flares. We would dress in one of two outfits: a hobo with an old hat, coat, and a beard drawn on by a burnt cork. Or a beatnik with an old beret and a baggy sweatshirt and a goatee also drawn on by a burnt cork.

Carrying an old pillowcase, we would hit each house shouting, "Help the poor!" just like our Catholic ancestors did hundreds of years ago in medieval Europe. Passing tons of other kids, we would stay out until every porch light was out. My pillowcase would be filled to the top when I finally returned. Best yet, no school tomorrow for all of us Catholic school kids. It was a holy day.

Kids in our neighborhood never knocked on doors or rang doorbells when we called on each other. That was for adults only. Instead, we went to the side door and shouted their names out over and over until they came out. "*Craige.*" "*Tome.*" "*Lee.*"

Two long blocks to the north were the stores. Everything you could ask for was lined up on Plymouth Road. Cunningham's for a jumbo malt (25 cents), Sanders for a hot fudge cream puff, Florsheim Shoes where we would get our feet x-rayed, Klein's Department Store where they would fly Santa Claus in a helicopter, and Woolworths for everything else.

Toys, models, hobbies, records, or whatever you wanted were at Woolworths Dime Store. Duncan yo-yos were the best yo-yos, and every summer, the Duncan Yo-yo Man would come and amaze us with his yo-yo tricks. Every winter, they would have a model custom car contest. We would buy a model car, take it home, and try our best to customize it, just like the custom cars in the magazines. If we managed to do a pretty good job, we would enter it in Woolworths contest. All the cars would be displayed in the front window where the blue ribbon winner would be king for a year. Woolworth always had the latest records (45s) in stock. I bought The Beatles's "I Want to Hold Your Hand" the day it came out.

A mile and a half down Plymouth Road was the Atlas Show where we saw every 1950s science fiction movie ever made. Some of my favorites were The Thing, The Blob, and Them. Great movies! I saw everyone on Saturday afternoon. The price was fifteen cents! I would get a quarter from my dad and be able to pay my admission to the show plus buy a small box of popcorn and a Slo Poke all-day sucker; all for a quarter! That was living! Then they raised the admission price to twenty-five cents! Yikes! Now I had to get thirty-five cents from the old man to keep up my Saturday afternoon lifestyle; not an easy task.

Sometimes I would walk to the show almost two miles away. I'm still amazed when I think back that I walked that far when I was young. One day when I was ten years old walking back from the Atlas, I got hit by a car. I was crossing Evergreen, and a teenager, driving a 51 Ford, hit me. I flew through the air, hit the ground, got up, and started to run. The teenager jumped out of his car, ran, and caught me.

"Let me go. I'm all right," I said.

"No, kid. You just got hit by a car. You've got to go to the hospital," he said.

I had a bump on my head, and my arm and knee were scraped. By now, a crowd had formed and then the cops pulled up in a snazzy new police car. Back then, the police cars were black with gold Detroit Police on the door. But this was a brand-new 1961 silver Plymouth with Detroit Police in blue letters, and a blue flasher on the roof.

The police officer told me this was a brand-new experimental design car, and I would be the first ever to ride in its back seat. Sometimes bad can turn to good. They put me in the back and drove me to Mount Carmel Hospital.

"Could you turn the new blue flasher on?" I asked.

He turned around and said, "No, kid. That's only for emergencies, and you're no emergency."

# Poland Comes Unraveled

THE YEAR 1683 WAS A dark time in Europe. The third and last crusade was going on, and the Ottoman Muslim Turks were at the gates of Vienna. The city had been besieged for two months. All the kings and nobles of Europe were terrified. If Vienna fell, all of Europe would fall, and this would be the end of Christianity. They needed a new leader and a new Army, so with hat in hand, they headed to Warsaw.

Poland amazingly had rebuilt itself from the horrible Swedish invasion it had endured just twenty-eight years earlier, and many of the rulers, who were heading to Warsaw, came from countries that helped Sweden in that invasion. One would think that these contemptible rulers would be too embarrassed to come crawling for help. But they were desperate, and they knew the Polish people were loyal and honorable and would never let the church they loved so much fall to the Ottomans.

King John Sobieski, who was elected king because of his great victories in battle, ruled Poland. King Sobieski formed an Army of Polish, German, and Austrian soldiers. The Polish cavalry, the greatest cavalry in the world, led them. The Polish cavalry wore feathers in their helmets, which expanded as they galloped, giving them a terrifying look. They carried long pikes and swords that they called Karabella; the best swords in Europe.

When Sobieski reached Vienna and was preparing for battle, a gift arrived. It was a large jar full of poppy seeds. It was from the commander of the Ottomans, Grand Vizier Kara Mustafa Pasha, with a note that read: for every seed in this jar, I have a man with a sword ready to fight! It was a clever symbol to scare Sobieski whose Army was greatly outnumbered. Sobieski emptied the jar and returned it with one red pepper inside.

Sobieski won the great battle and saved European Christianity. The date of the battle was September 11 (911). That's a date every American knows. What a coincidence the Christian Polish Army beat the Muslim Turks on September 11, 1683. Then a few hundred years later on the very same date, Muslim terrorists destroy the World Trade Center. I learned this when I attended a New York firefighter's funeral right after 911. It was at St Patrick's Cathedral in Manhattan, and Cardinal Edward Egan mentioned it in his stirring eulogy. How amazing the history of Poland is.

The fleeing Turks did leave a gift. In their haste, they dropped bags of coffee beans. Nobody knew what they were until some captured Turks showed them how to brew coffee. That was why Vienna became the coffee capital of Europe. Sobieski brought some of those coffee beans back to Poland, and to this very day, Polish people are also big coffee drinkers.

Poland's great victory in Vienna was a high point in her history rightly so, but it also turned out to be the beginning of the end. Poland's government proved unworkable due to the Librium Veto where any one member could stop any legislation. They called it their golden freedom where the rich landowners had no rules, and the peasants had no rights. Chaos and backwardness took over, and nothing could be done about it.

Poland's neighbors, who quickly forgot about how Poland saved Europe from the invading Muslims, began to take advantage of the situation. They made deals with the Polish aristocrats who quickly sold out their country to the Russians, Germans, and Austrians. In 1772 came the first of three partitions. Poland lost one third of her country to Russia, Germany, and Austria

America was fighting her own revolution at about this time, and two very famous generals left Poland and joined her fight. The first was Casimir Pulaski, who is also known as the father of American cavalry, and he fought bravely for the Americans. He was killed in 1779 during the battle of Savannah.

Thaddeus Kosciuszko, the other Polish general who joined America's fight, is known as the father of American artillery. As an engineer, he designed and built an impregnable fort on the banks of the Hudson River called West Point, home to America's Military Academy. After the revolutionary war, Kosciuszko returned to Poland and led an Army against the countries that were trying to take her over.

In 1791, Poland passed the very first constitution in Europe. It was patterned after America's Constitution, the only other country in the world to have a constitution. It gave freedom to all Polish people, rich and poor alike. This enraged Russia who would not stand for free Polish peasants just across the border from her enslaved peasants. In 1792, Russia attacked Poland.

General Kosciuszko formed an Army of free peasants and nobles who fought together for the first time. It took all three countries, Russia, Germany, and Austria, to defeat them. As usual, nobody came to Poland's aid. In 1795, Poland lost and was partitioned for the third and final time. After over eight hundred years of proud history, Poland was erased off the map.

The Russians and Germans outlawed everything Polish. Schools could not teach in Polish. Names of towns were changed from Polish names to German- and Russian-sounding names.

For 123 years until 1918, Polish people did not have a country. My relatives told me horror stories of Russian Cossacks murdering, raping, and robbing people. The Polish people back in Poland resisted the best they could. In 1797, Jozef Wybicki wrote the Polish national anthem, *Poland Is Not Yet Lost*. In it, they sing, "March, march, Dombrowski." It is a song about a great Polish general who formed an Army to free Poland. In 1831, during another uprising, the Polish red-and-white flag first appeared.

It was in this period of time that most of our Polish ancestors immigrated to America. "We left hell and arrived in heaven," my grandmother would say. No young Polish American was ever told anything good about Poland by his or her grandparents. We were told that it was a place of hunger, fear, poverty, and oppression. Unlike other nationalities where young folks hear beautiful stories of their native land, we never did. Instead, our parents taught us how great this country is and how lucky we are to live here. America became our new home, and nobody loves America more than the Polish!

# Coming to America

ALL FOUR OF MY GRANDPARENTS came from the Russian-controlled section of Poland, and all four of my grandparents immigrated to the US in the early part of the twentieth century. My grandfather, Stanislaw Dombrowski, was the first. He arrived in the Port of Baltimore on November 24, 1903.

My grandfather Stanislaw was of noble class; a small-time noble but still a noble, unlike my three other grandparents who were of solid peasant class. My grandfather Stanislaw Dombrowski was what the Spanish call a hidalgo: a noble with no money but a good name and a horse, except I don't think he had a horse.

So like most Polish Americans, I come mainly from peasant stock, which is a good thing. Most nobles had it good in Poland even under the occupation, so they stayed. The peasants had it bad, so they left. Therefore, the peasant grandchildren, like myself, were raised in the land of milk and honey while the nobles' grandchildren dealt with the horrors of the Nazis and later the communists.

Stanislaw, like so many other Poles, headed west to the coal mines of Western Pennsylvania. He sent for his wife, Mary, who came through Ellis Island with two little girls in tow, my aunt Genevieve and my aunt Lottie. They all settled in Forest City, Pennsylvania, where for the next eighteen years, my grandfather worked the coal mines where he got black lung disease. They also brought six more children into this world: Helen, Barney, Wesley, Chester (my father), Edmund, and Eugene.

In 1918, the Dombrowskis did what so many other people were doing. They left the coal mines and headed for the factories of

Detroit. Grandpa Stanly got a job at the Packard Automotive Plant on East Grand Boulevard. Today it is one of the largest vacant structures in the world. Grandpa Stanly worked there for eleven years until the crash of September 1929 when he and millions of other Americans lost their jobs. My grandfather never worked another day in his life.

This would become the family conflict; that my grandfather didn't work. My father and his brothers would never talk about their dad. They resented him to the point of hatred as much as they loved their mother. I understand Polish people believe in work. We detest slackers and people who don't work. But I also understand that my grandfather was fifty-five when he lost his job, and during the Great Depression, it must have been pretty hard for a fifty-five-year-old man who couldn't speak a word of English and had black lung disease to find a job.

Although Grandpa had no job and no money, it didn't stop the old hidalgo from living the noble life. He never left the house without a coat and tie and usually accompanied with a derby and spats. He would walk around the West Side Polonia talking to everyone tipping his derby and doing a European curtsy for the ladies. Grandpa also liked his beer. I understand how this bothered my dad and his brothers who were raised by their mother to be humble hard workers and mostly teetotalers.

I only saw two pictures of my grandfather, probably the only two ever taken of him. In one picture, he and another gentleman are sitting at a kitchen table drinking a beer. The other picture is when he was lying in his coffin. In both pictures, he wore a coat and tie.

As lazy as my one grandfather was said to be, my other grandfather was said to be a very hard worker. Anthony and Victoria Slawek and their daughter Lillian, arrived in America in 1913. Anthony was thirty-one, Victoria was twenty-six, and Aunt Lillian was two. They came straight to Detroit and rented a place in West Side Polonia at 1256 Central Avenue. Grandpa Anthony was also a miner but in the salt mines under Detroit. On weekends, he would take the train to Jackson where he shared a small farm and grew all his vegetables. When probation came, he did well making bathtub gin. My mom would tell me how scared she was when he took her with him at night to dispose of the mash.

"It was always late at night. Pa would load up his old cart with all the mash from cooking his gin. Then the two of us would go to a dumpsite and get rid of the mash. I would be so scared the police would see us, but they never did. It was frightening, but I always liked helping Pa out," she told me.

Grandpa Anthony built his own house: a big white, two flat on Chopin Street. Altogether, they would have six kids: Lillian, Cassie, Casimir, Henrietta (my mom), Hank, and Irene. Life was good for the Slawek's until 1934 when Grandpa got a hernia while working at the farm. He died on the way to the hospital. Don't ever tell me hard work never killed anyone. My mom told me his funeral was so big that the Detroit Police sent two motorcycle cops to escort it and that was before most people even had a car. Grandpa was well liked. He ran his little speakeasy in his basement, and he was very handy. Folks often came to him when they needed help.

But that was it for the Slaweks. There were no pensions or social security back then. They lost everything including the house. The older ones went off and got married, leaving my mom, Uncle Hank, and Aunt Irene, along with Grandma to fend for themselves. But there was no fending.

The depression was going on. My mom and dad and most other people who were living in the old Polish neighborhoods were poor and living in poverty. They would tell me stories of no heat in the winter, and nothing to eat. They would go to the fire station, Ladder 22 on McGraw, for a free bowl of soup. On Christmas, the Salvation Army would bring them a little box. In it would be a pair of socks, a book, and some hard candy. That's all they got, and they were happy to get it. For that reason, I will always support the Salvation Army. These are the stories that all of us Polish baby boomers grew up hearing. And they made us appreciate so much more everything we had, even if it wasn't a whole lot.

They also taught us to appreciate the old west side neighborhood, which we would call Michigan and Central. I loved going down there to visit my grandmother and many other relatives. They had a bar or a bakery on every corner, often with a candy store next door. The houses had little manicured lawns, spotlessly painted big front porches, and little gardens with a bird bath in every backyard.

Sometimes Mom and I would walk up to the stores on Michigan Avenue to pick up a few things. We would walk along Michigan Avenue, stopping in every store. Most of the stores and restaurants had Polish names, and the people spoke Polish. All the stores smelled so good! From one of the many Polish butchers, Mom would buy kielbasa, city chicken (cut-up pieces of pork and veil on small wooden skewers; why it was called city chicken, nobody knows), and the freshest lunch meat ever. At the bakery, Mom would buy Polish rye with seeds and chrusciki (angel wings) and sometimes mariannes, inverted cupcakes covered in raspberry jelly and coconut with whipped cream on top. Yum!

Streetcars would be clinking up and down Michigan. My dad was always going to take me for a ride on one and then one day they were all gone! I never got that ride. We would pass by the many bars that lined Michigan. On nice days, the front doors were wide open, and the aroma of whiskey greeted us as I sneaked a peek inside to see all the men bellied up to the bar downing their ice-cold boombas.

Sometimes we would walk all the way to the Senate Theater where on one side they had the Senate Sweet Shop, and on the other side was the Senate Coney Island. Detroit is the Coney Island capital of America: chili dogs, but really, really good chili dogs.

Downtown Detroit has the two original Coney Island restaurants: Lafayette Coney Island and American Coney Island. They are right next door to each other. Every Detroiter has a favorite, Lafayette or American, except for us West Side Polish people. To us, the argument was Senate Coney Island or George's Coney Island. Those two Coney Islands were a block apart on Michigan Avenue. Senate had a little more modern layout, post-World War II, but George's was right out of the 1920s. Plain white walls with wooden tables and chairs. Men waiters would bring us hot chili in white bowls and coffee in heavy white mugs. Both restaurants were great. Mom and I liked Senate, but Dad liked George's.

# Good Humor Man

DETROIT IN THE FIFTIES WAS a very prosperous city; one of the most prosperous in America, even in the world. Our fathers would all go off to work at the car companies and all day our streets would fill with different men trying to sell us things, trying to get their own little piece of the American dream.

We had a man for everything bringing us everything, mainly made in Detroit. A milkman, an egg man, a bread man, a potato chip man (Superior Potato Chips were the freshest chips ever, made the same day that they were delivered.), a knife-sharpening man, a fruit-and-vegetable man, a sheeny man (looking for junk), a Hudson's man (the green trucks that were so familiar delivering all the goods people bought the day before), the Koenig coal man (some folks still heated with coal), the popcorn man (the aroma of freshly popped popcorn), and last but not least, my favorite, the Good Humor man.

Good Humor was not the only ice cream trucks that roamed our streets trying to get our nickels and dimes in exchange for their frozen treats. We had Mr. Softie, Jolly Popsicles, Dixie Cone, and so on, but the best, the gourmet of ice cream bars was Good Humor.

We rarely got a Good Humor. They were expensive at fifteen cents. The truck would glide right by us ringing its bells. Except for the Krandull kids: two spoiled brats who had a built-in pool in their backyard. They would hold a little lottery every afternoon to see which of us kids would get to swim in their pool. I never bothered; I just grabbed my rolled up towel and headed to Rouge Pools.

The Good Humor man would stop every day in front of the Krandulls. As the two boys made their decision, we watched and thought the way all kids that want something they can't afford think, *How can I get me some of that?* One day, we figured a way. There was a flaw in the Good Humor vehicle. And I figured it out.

The Good Humor truck was a custom-made white truck with a driver's seat and an open top. Behind the driver was a box filled with ice cream and dry ice. The box had a door on the side and a door in the very back. Below that back door was the rear bumper. That was the flaw! A person could jump up on that back bumper when the driver wasn't looking, open that back door, and help himself to all the ice cream he wanted, jumping off at the next stop. I told my friends.

From that moment on, every time the Good Humor man came down the street, we had a new way of looking at it. It was an opportunity just waiting for us. As it passed by, we would look at each other with that secret grin that all robbers have as they case their next joint. Day by day as the truck passed by, our smile would grow a little smaller because we knew we didn't really have the guts to pull it off. Then one day, we told Conrad.

Conrad wasn't like the rest of us. He was a couple of years older and tougher than anybody on the block and half crazy. Nobody messed with Conrad.

As the Good Humor truck passed by, Conrad laughed and said, "Let's do it."

"You mean right now, Conrad?" I asked.

"Yes, right now, you punks."

And the three of us started running down Patton. Tommy and I didn't know what to think. We never did anything like this before. We stole popcorn out of the machines in the park, like everybody else and maybe a quarter out of our mom's purse, but this was big time.

The truck stopped for a customer, and sure as heck, Conrad jumped on the back and opened the door. The truck was moving along as Conrad reached in and pulled out a whole box, tucked it under his arm, and got ready to jump.

But the truck didn't stop. It rolled the stop sign at West Chicago and made a left and headed off with Conrad holding on. Tommy and I ran along as fast as we could, not knowing Conrad's fate. Maybe it was heading all the way back to the ice cream factory. What would Conrad do?

Just then, Conrad jumped and did a 180 somersault on West Chicago. He got up scraped and bruised from head to foot. Conrad didn't feel pain like the rest of us. With a pissed off look on his face and a box of Good Humors under his arm, Conrad walked up to us.

"Look what happened to me because of you two punks' stupid idea. I ought to kick both of your asses! I'm eating this whole box of Good Humors myself. You're not getting one!"

Tommy and I didn't say anything. We just walked back with Conrad. Then Conrad opened up the box and handed Tommy and I one each. They were toasted coconuts. Yum! Conrad was like that. He pushed us around, but you could always depend on him for a favor or an ice cream. My parents always told me that you could never enjoy something stolen, but they tasted pretty good to me.

I decided right then that life of crime was not for me, and at twelve years old, I got a paper route. That would be my first of an uninterrupted forty-eight years of work. I had bought my own shoes since the age of twelve. My dad got me the paper route. He bowled with a guy at Crown Lanes who managed the newspaper station. The guy's name was The Dude, and he fit it well. Dude had greased back hair and wore big pointed shoes. He drove a 1950 Mercury (like the car James Dean drove in the movie *Rebel Without a Cause*). It was lowered to the ground and painted dark green. It had a woodpecker smoking a cigar decal on the side fender and loud Hollywood mufflers. It was the total picture of cool.

The Dude ran the Detroit News station that was located behind the candy store at Plymouth Road and Plainview. At that time, Detroit had two newspapers: the Detroit News and the Detroit Free Press. We had a third paper: the Detroit Times, which folded up in 1960. The big difference with the two papers was that the Free Press was a morning paper, and the News was an afternoon paper. That affected everything from the editorials to who read the paper to who delivered the papers.

The Free Press paperboys had to get up at five every morning seven days a week. No way could I ever manage that. We delivered the News at a much more reasonable time: after school, except on weekends when we also delivered the papers early. On Saturdays, we had to deliver the paper twice: mornings and early evenings when we would deliver the bulldogs, an early edition of the Sunday morning paper. It was a lot of work for a twelve-year-old kid. On Sunday mornings, if I overslept, Dude would personally deliver the papers to my house for a small charge. Dude's loud Hollywood mufflers would awaken me. He would drop off my papers while yelling out the window. "You owe me fifty cents!"

We delivered the papers on our bikes, rain, snow, or sunshine. They gave us a canvas bag with The Detroit News written in red letters that we hooked to our handlebars and held in place by an ingeniously designed metal bar. I would ride down the sidewalk holding the handlebar with my left hand while throwing the rolled up paper with my right. It seemed to never land on the porch, usually the bushes.

The Detroit News had a big promotion to sign up new customers. They even brought in a good speaker to get us all fired up, and there would be prizes for whoever signed up the most new customers. I was pumped! I hit every noncustomer on my route using all the speaker's talking points. "If you just cut out the coupons, the paper more than pays for itself!" Sayings like that got me eleven new customers. Most stopped after the promotion. But it paid off. I signed up enough to win a football!

They never gave me the football. They kept it at the station to kill time whenever the paper truck was late. I didn't care. We would have touch football games on the street as we waited. When the papers arrived, we would roll them up on the benches and then shove them in our bags for delivery. But you had to watch out. It seemed a few guys had a couple of extra customers that the News didn't know about, so they would be short on papers and looked for a couple to swipe. If they couldn't swipe yours, then they would raid the paper boxes on Plymouth Road.

After delivering papers at thirteen, I entered the retail business. I got a job at Rouge Park Beer and Wine Store on West Chicago. Back then, every beer store had a kid to carry out the cases of beer. The customer would pull up, I would get the empties out of his trunk, then get a case out of the back cooler and load it into his trunk.

Detroit used to have five breweries downtown. Stroh's, Goebel, Pfeiffer, Altes, and E & B were all brewed in Detroit. Those five beers along with Pabst and Blatz were called local and sold for around $3.50 a case plus deposit. Miller and Budweiser were premium back then and cost a little more.

Around four in the afternoon, we would get a rush. Inner city men who worked in the factories on Plymouth Road, would stop in on their way home. They pulled up in their Olds '98s or their Buick Electra 225s (Deuce and a Quarter) and asked for the same thing, "A tall Bud and a pack of Kools, my man." Then they hopped into their car, dropped the top, turned up the music (Motown), lit up a Kool, opened their Bud, and headed east on Chicago.

"Hey, how about a ride?" I'd yell.

"Tomorrow," they would yell back as they pulled away. Of course, tomorrow never came.

Johnny, who had the Shell station across the street, came in one day and asked me if I wanted a job pumping gas. This was back before people pumped their own gas. "Sure. Who wouldn't?" I said.

The Shell station was a hip spot and everyone in the neighborhood with a cool car went there for gas, and I loved cool cars. I pumped their gas, cleaned their windshield, checked the oil and the tires, then collected the two bucks for the gas, and say "Thank you, ma'am or sir." It was a good job.

It's funny when I think back about my first three jobs growing up in Detroit. None of them are there today. People often talk about all the factory jobs that left the city, but they should also remember that a lot of jobs that young people had left too.

# THE GREAT WAR

WORLD WAR I OR THE Great War started on July 28, 1914, when the Austrian-Hungarian Empire declared war on Serbia. Exactly one month earlier on June 28, a terrorist named Gavril Principe shot and killed the Austrian Archduke Franz Ferdinand and his wife in Sarajevo, setting the stage for this horrific event. All of Europe took sides with Russia, England, and France forming an alliance called the Triple Entente versus Germany, Austria, Hungary, and the Ottomans who called themselves the Central Powers.

They say on that day, July 28, 1914, the centers of every city in Europe were filled with people waving flags cheering for the new war. Nobody wanted to be left out. This time, they would show the whole world that you don't mess with the Germans or the French or the Bosnians or any other nationality that was out there cheering. Fools they all were. Over the next four years, millions would die, and nations would be wiped off the map. Not surprising, they weren't cheering in Warsaw or any of the other Polish cities.

Poland still did not have a country; worse yet, they were divided three ways with the Russian section fighting with the Triple Entente and the German and Austrian sections fighting with the Central Powers. It would be brother versus brother; they would be drafted to defend the honor of kings who had no honor for them.

Much of the fighting on the eastern front took place in Poland. Many towns, homes, and farms were destroyed. Two million Polish fought in the war and 450,000 were killed. To encourage the Poles to fight on their side, all three kings offered them freedom if their side should win. But most Poles knew better. Winners never give up anything.

Then in 1917, two events happened that changed the course of history for Poland and the war: the Russians had a revolution, and America entered the war. America stayed out of the war for the first three years; in fact, President Wilson ran for reelection in 1916 with the slogan, "He kept us out of that European War!" Then Wilson got reelected and changed his mind. In 1917, the USA began sending over ten thousand troops a day to Europe.

Wilson also had a fourteen-point peace plan; the thirteenth of which gave Poland back her country. Much of the credit for this was that the Polish people in America were organizing and forming political groups and began pressuring President Wilson who was a Democrat as were most of the Polish at that time. At first, Wilson was hesitant to support a free Poland because part of Poland belonged to Russia, one of our allies. But the Russian Revolution solved that problem.

The Germans and the Russians were fighting each other in Russian Poland. The Germans drove the Russians all the way back to Russia when the communists took over. Vladimir Lenin, who now headed Russia and feared a German invasion, sued for peace. In 1917, the Germans and the Russians signed the Treaty of Brest Litovsk, which gave all of Russian Poland to Germany. So now, Poland was just divided in two: between Germany and Austria.

Now that Russia was out of it, the Polish people had just one enemy: the Central Powers. The Polish formed their own Army called Haller's Blue Army named after their leader, General Józef Haller von Hallenburg; a Pole with a German-sounding name. They were called blue because they wore blue uniforms. Sixty-five thousand Polish from all over Europe joined along with twenty-three thousand from America.

The Blue Army fought on the western front alongside the French. On November 11, 1918, the war ended with America being on the victorious side, and as promised by President Wilson, Poland got her country back. Five days later on November 16, 1918, Poland declared her independence.

But it wasn't easy, the countries that had controlled Poland for over a 123 years didn't leave peacefully. No, they fought on. The Ukraine attacked Poland, and the German soldiers still in Poland fought the Polish. In the spring of 1919, Haller's Blue Army was sent to Poland. They fought with the local Poles and defeated the Ukrainians and drove the Germans back to Germany and then in 1920 came the Polish-Russian War!

In what many historians say is one of the most important and overlooked wars of the twentieth century, Poland and Soviet Russia went to war over border disputes. But Russia had much more in mind. Vladimir Lenin and the communists won the Russian Revolution. He then wanted to take his workers revolution to the rest of Europe. Workers throughout Europe were sympathetic to Communism. Many were tired of living like peasants as the rich got richer, and after four years of war and millions dead, many people were looking for change. Germany was going through its own revolution, and the commies were gaining the upper hand. The timing was right for Lenin and his Red Army to try to take over Europe, and the first stop was Poland.

The Russian and Polish armies met at the border, and Russia drove the Poles all the way back to Warsaw. It looked grim for the Polish. England tried to send their surplus World War I military equipment to Poland, but the English dockworkers who were pro-communist refused to load it onto ships. The badly needed equipment sat there on the docks. All over Europe, many workers were rooting for the communists.

Poland needed a miracle, and they got one called the Miracle at Vistula. First, Poland broke the Russian code. No people on earth are better code breakers than the Polish. Knowing the Russian plans, Poland strategically attacked the Russians and drove them all the way back to Russia in one of the greatest battles in history. Soviet Russia and Lenin sued for peace in the Treaty of Riga, and the borders were set, at least until the next war. The Polish won a great victory and saved the Europeans from communism but as usual never received the recognition they deserved.

# Club 1270

We had a couple of after-school TV shows everyone watched: *Club 1270* and *Swingin' Time.* They were both really good local versions of American Bandstand. Detroit was loaded with talent back then. We had all the Motown stars plus Mitch Ryder and Bob Seger and tons of others.

Some of my buddies had older sisters. They would get together after school, turn on the TV (black and white) to channel 7 for Club 1270 or channel 9 for Swingin' Time, and dance away, usually line dances, while my buddies and I would sit on the sofa and make fun of them.

Many of the teen dancers on the TV shows, especially Club 1270, lived in our neighborhood, so after the show was over, we could walk up to the stores and see our TV stars hanging out in front of Cunningham's Drugstore acting normal just like all the other neighborhood juvenile delinquents. How cool was that!

On the corner of Braille and Plymouth was a soft-serve ice-cream place called Twin Kiss. Jamie Coe the singer owned it. When he wasn't making hit records like "The Fool" or doing shows at the clubs, he was behind the window making milkshakes. We had a 1960s musicale neighborhood in what many people called America's Most Musical City!

At about this time a new kid moved into the neighborhood from the old West Side Polish neighborhood named Johnny K. Johnny K was the Fonzie times two. He wore tight pants and big-pointed shoes and had greased back hair. He immediately took over the neighborhood. On his first day at school, he kicked the butt of what was one of the toughest kids in school. After that, nobody messed with Johnny. He was a teacher. He taught us how to dress, smoke cigarettes, and how to play mumblety-peg with a pocketknife. Johnny also brought with him two gorgeous sisters named Marilyn and Sherry.

Marilyn was our age, and Sherry was a couple of years older, old enough to go out with boys in cars, and every boy in the neighborhood with a car wanted to go out with her. One day after school, Danny and I were sitting on the couch in Johnny's living room watching Club 1270. Sherry and Marilyn and a couple of other older neighborhood girls were dancing along with the TV. The song "Do I Love You" by The Ronettes came on. Sherry stopped dancing, knelt down in front of us, and very sexually, pantomimed the whole song! Wow! It's moments like that which stay with a young man forever.

Being Polish meant being with your relatives a lot. No holiday or birthday or weekend went by without your aunts, uncles, and cousins stopping by or vice versa. Most of my relatives lived in Detroit or Downriver. Our two closest relatives were the Elinskis who lived just south of Joy, and the Darrys who lived just the other side of the park.

The Darrys were originally named Dombrowskis. Back in the 40s and 50s, a lot of Polish people changed their ethnic last names to American-sounding ones. It was the thing to do. The entire family wanted to look and sound as American as we could. All the Dombrowskis got together and tried to pick out a new last name that they could agree on. Uncle Wesley liked the name Darry. I never knew why and neither did the rest of the family. So he became Darry, and the rest of the family stayed Dombrowski. That was the closest we came to changing our Polish last name. I'm glad we didn't.

My aunt and uncle's kids had grown and left. They were empty nesters. I could stay there whenever I wanted, and I did, sometimes for weeks at a time. They would let me stay up and watch TV as late as I wanted, which was great especially on Friday nights when *Shock Theatre* was on! "Lock your doors, turn off your lights, and turn up the TV. It's time for Shock Theatre!" I'd sit there watching a scary black-and-white movie with a big bowl of popcorn that Aunt Cassie popped for me.

They lived on Parkland across from Rouge Park. Right across from their house sat the Army's Nike missiles. These tall white rockets that would pop out of the ground and dare any Russian bomber to fly over Detroit.

Rouge Park was full of Army stuff. We had the Nike missile base, silver Quonset huts by the toboggan slides where the soldiers lived, a big rotating radar unit on the corner of Joy Road and Outer Drive that made the car's radio beep whenever we rode past, and green Army jeeps full of soldiers cruising Outer Drive. Yep, our neighborhood was very much part of the Cold War.

Downtown was the place to be growing up in Detroit, especially in the early 60s. Starting at around age thirteen, I would head downtown every chance I had. We could take the West Chicago or Joy Road or Plymouth Road bus and then transfer to other buses, sometimes as many as three until we got Downtown. It was our big city adventure, about a twelve-mile ride. It was exciting and safe. Our parents never worried.

A bus ride on the DSR was a quarter plus a dime for a transfer, fifty cents got us into the Fox theatre, and seventy-five cents got us a bleacher seat in Tiger Stadium. Sliders cost twelve cents, or I could get a Coney for a quarter. So if I had a couple of bucks, I could have a big time in our big city.

Friday after Thanksgiving, Downtown would be packed. The sidewalks were almost impassable. The stores would also be packed with shoppers, and Santa's ringing bells on every corner. Good luck finding an empty seat at the lunch counter at Kresge's five-and-dime store or anywhere else Downtown.

The crown jewel of Downtown was Hudson's, one of the biggest department stores in the world. This massive 410-foot brick palace on Woodward Avenue with over two million square feet of shopping, centered right in the heart of Downtown Detroit. Inside was every item known to modern man: from shoes to hats, from toys to furniture, from soup to Maurice salads.

The first thing we did when we got to Hudson's was walk around on the store's heated sidewalks and check out all the window displays. They would be decorated for Christmas with mechanical elves building toys for the children. Once inside, we would be blown away by the holiday excitement everyone had. We then would take the elevator up to the twelfth floor for Toyland and check out the Lionel train layout, the very best in the land.

Lionel trains were king. Every boy in Detroit had a set in his basement, usually on top of an old drafting board. Some kids had incredible layouts that their dads built, but most of us had a pretty basic layout. It didn't matter. They were our pride and joy.

But cars were always number one to Detroit boys. All winter, we would build model cars in our basement while reading Hot Rod and Car Craft magazines. Then as March approached, America's greatest hot rod show *Autorama* would come to Downtown Detroit at Cobo Hall.

We would take the bus to Cobo and hang out at the Autorama all day and night, looking at the coolest creations of mankind. George Barris, Big Daddy Roth, and Detroit's own, Alexander Brothers, would display their latest creations of chopped-and-channeled metallic-painted and chromed four-hundred-horsepower masterpieces! We would look and marvel right until the show closed, and they threw us out. Then we took the bus home.

We left Cobo, walked to Woodward, and caught the Woodward bus to Warren Avenue. This would not be my normal way home, but my friend who I was with, Gary, lived on Tireman, so we rode the Warren bus to Patton, and I would walk home from there. But this time, we screwed up and mistakenly caught the East Warren bus and rode it until it ended somewhere around Grosse Pointe.

When the bus stopped, we told the driver our mistake. "No problem," he said and gave us new transfers. "Just wait for the bus that says Crosstown, and it will take you where you want to go. He gave us good advice, and before I knew it, I was getting off at Patton and then ran the last mile and half home. When I got home, the door was unlocked, and everyone was sleeping. Mom left a light on.

It was after midnight, and I was only thirteen. I couldn't imagine that happening in today's world; unsupervised thirteen-year-olds at midnight riding a Downtown bus, but that was how things were when I grew up, and it was okay.

# POLISH WEDDINGS

HERE ARE SOME FUN FACTS about weddings in Poland. They throw oats and barley at the newlyweds instead of rice. During communist time, Polish people had to get married twice, first in the Catholic Church and second at city hall because the communist government did not recognize the Church.

In the old days, Polish people went to great lengths to let the world know they had a suitable daughter. They would decorate the house with wreaths and special colors of paint. In Krakow, for example, they would paint the whole house light blue.

When a suitable boy saw this, he would have to go to the town's intermediary, a babcia or wise woman, to intervene with the girl's family. This could save him a lot of embarrassment. If the girl's family approved of him, he would be invited over for dinner. He would bring a bottle of vodka decorated with flowers. He would sit at the table and the girl would come out and they would meet for the first time. He would then ask the girl for a glass. She would leave the room. If she returned with a glass, he was in. If she didn't return, he was out. I guess he would then leave with his bottle of vodka and drown his sorrows.

How did Polish weddings get so famous in America? They even made a movie in 1998 called *Polish Wedding* filmed in Hamtramck, Michigan. It was the actress Kristen Bell's (who is from Detroit and also Polish) first film. She had a small role and didn't get any credit.

The truth is that most people, including Polish people, have never been to a traditional Polish wedding. Nowadays, Polish people have weddings just like everyone else's unless it's at a Polish hall with Polish food. But it didn't used to be that way.

When our grandparents got married back in Poland, the weddings were three days long. They were mostly peasant farmers, and folks traveled long ways to attend a wedding, so they had to stay three days. The bride's and groom's families would put them up and feed them for the three days, and the tradition started. When our grandparents arrived here in America, and their children got married, they tried as best they could to carry on the old world Polish tradition.

When I was a child in the 1950s, many of the weddings were still three days long. Weddings were always held on Saturday, so Friday would be the church rehearsal followed with a big rehearsal dinner. That would be day one.

Saturday was the big day. The church ceremony would always be on Saturday and in the morning. The bride would leave from her parents and walk to church. She would be accompanied by her parents, her maid of honor, bridesmaids, and lots of other people including musicians and always an accordion player who would serenade her as she walked. Catholic churches in old Polish neighborhoods were seldom more than a few blocks away.

How happy everyone would be as they walked along. The bridesmaids would hold up the back of the bride's gown. Little children dressed in their best would run along, and everyone would be laughing. All the neighbors would be out on their porches, waving and shouting congratulations. "Good luck, Wanda. Have fun. We love you!" they said as they proceeded to the church. What a great way to start a wedding day.

Church would be the usual Catholic wedding mass with communion. This was back when we had to fast before receiving communion, so everyone was starving when mass ended. The bride and groom came out to a shower of rice. Then the party headed to breakfast.

The halls of choice for West Siders were Dom Polski on Junction or Martin Hall on Martin. Polish people, especially men, do not like to eat on an empty stomach, especially on a wedding Saturday. No worry because the first thing they saw waiting for them as they walked in the hall were long tables set up with dozens of pitchers of cold beer and literally hundreds of poured shots of whiskey. There was no waiting for drinks.

When breakfast started, piles of food would be served including kielbasa, fresh and smoked, scrambled eggs, and everything else. We would eat away, stopping only for the banging of silverware on the plates, a signal for the newlyweds to kiss. The bride would keep her veil on the whole time. The band would play softly in the background. It was an all-day gig for them. After breakfast, everyone would return home for a nap, so they were ready for the evening festivities.

Walking back into that hall that evening would be so exciting. Hundreds of people, most of your relatives dressed in their best, loudly talking and laughing, drinks in everyone's one hand, and usually a cigarette or cigar hanging out of their mouth. "Hey, Bobby, come over give your aunt a kiss." Then my aunt would bend over and plant some red lipstick on my check. My uncles with their cigars in their mouth would reach out and shake my hand and say "What grade are you in now?" or "Where's your dad?"

"Dinner served!" Everyone would head to the downstairs dining room. There would be long dining tables with white paper tablecloths, plates and silverware, baskets of good Polish rye bread, and butter dishes with ice cubes to keep the butter cold. I jumped up on my wooden folding seat and the food came rolling out. Salad, potatoes, vegetables, pierogies, then roast beef and gravy, more kielbasa, chicken, and of course, city chicken, a Detroit favorite that has no chicken in it. Delicious! Then we would have dessert, usually apple pie. Wedding cake would be saved for later.

We ate until we couldn't move, stopping only for the usual banging of silverware on plates signaling for the bride, still in her veil, and groom to kiss. After eating, we would all head back upstairs to the Polish ballroom. Let the party begin!

The evening festivities would start with the oczepiny, the unveiling of the bride. Everyone would form a circle around the bride. Her mother and bridesmaids would be alongside her and help as she removed her veil. Then she would put an apron on (this was the fifties). Now, voilà! She was a married woman. Let the party begin.

The music, polkas, and more polkas, a little rock and roll, a little jazz, and of course, the *Hokey Pokey* would start, and the dance floor would fill up. All Polish women love to dance. Polish men come in two types. Either they love to dance, or they never dance, nothing in between. My uncle Ted was the best polka dancer ever. He would glide across the floor as his feet moved like a flamenco dancer, and he was a big guy, a paratrooper during the war.

While Uncle Ted, my dad, and the other men who liked to dance could have all the dance partners they wanted, the women weren't as lucky, so they would dance with each other, or worse yet, dance with us. My aunts would drag my cousins and I out on the floor, and away we would go to the beat of some crazy polka.

As the evening went on, the hall would get so hot, but that wouldn't slow down the party one beat. The windows would open, suit coats off, ties off, and white shirtsleeves rolled up. The music got louder, and the cold beer flowed. Around midnight, they would cut the cake. Pieces of cake were wrapped in wedding napkins and given to each person to take home. Young girls would put the cake under their pillow. Legend said that they would dream of their future husband.

Sunday was the poprawiny (pronounced popraveeneh). All Polish people know what that means. We gather and eat and drink all the leftovers. Although after most weddings it was all freshly cooked, little would be left after a Polish wedding. It was usually held at the house of the bride's family, and the place would be packed top to bottom. It was another day of eating and drinking and merriment!

The women would usually fill the basement while the men sat out back smoking their White Owls or RG Duns and drinking their cold Strohs or Pabst beers. They would talk about sports or politics or their job at the shop. It was always called the shop, never the factory or the plant or anything else, just the shop. The newlyweds would happily stroll through as everyone joked with them and asked about their plans.

As evening rolled in, folks would slowly get up and head home. Monday morning came early, and everyone had work to do, but they all had a break from it and a wonderful three days.

# POLISH MUSIC

WHAT'S MORE POLISH THEN THE polka? Polish festivals, Polish weddings, or Polish anything, polka music is always played. But many historians claim the polka isn't Polish and was not started by the Polish. No, they claim the Czechs started it. I don't agree.

They say a young girl named Anna Slezakova, who was a housemaid, started the polka dance in 1830 in the town of Tynec Nad Labem in Bohemia. She originally called the dance the madera. This, according to a story first published in Bohemia in 1894, sixty-four years after the fact.

But how did the word madera get changed to polka? The entomology of a word, or what language the word is in, is a very important factor when determining where something originated. The word polka has no meaning in the Czech language. In Polish, the word polka means Polish woman. So why would the Czechs name the dance Polish woman? Maybe they didn't!

The biggest reason that I say the polka is Polish is that the polka that we know is a unique American style. It is only danced in America, not in Europe. Nobody in Czech or Poland dances the polka the same way we do. American-style polka was started by Polish immigrants in cities like Detroit and Chicago back in the 1920s and is still danced today by the Polish.

In Chicago, they have The International Polka Association or the IPA. It is an organization dedicated to preserve Polish-heritage polkas. They hold a convention every year, usually in Polish cities like Buffalo, New York, Chicago, or Detroit. They have a Polka Hall of Fame started in 1969; the first two winners were Frankie Yankovic and Lil Wally Jagiello. If you have never heard of either of those two, then you're not Polish.

Also in Polish communities throughout America, we have Polish festivals featuring polka dancing. Some of the bigger Detroit festivals are the following:

The Hamtramck Labor Day Festival in Hamtramck
The Sweetest Heart of Mary Pierogi Festival in Detroit
American Polish Century Club's Polish Festival in Sterling Heights
Orchard Lake Saint Mary's Polish Festival in Orchard Lake
Our Lady of Scapular's Polish Festival in Wyandotte

I don't see other nationalities having polka festivals with the polka tents like we do. So from this day on, never let anyone say the polka isn't Polish. Yes, the polka is Polish, and more importantly it is Polish American, and it is owned by the Polish Americans lock stock and barrel, beer barrel that is.

Polish people, like most Europeans, love classical music. The greatest piano composer to ever live came from Poland. His name was Frederic Chopin. In Poland, they say, "To know the Polish people, you must know Chopin."

Frederic Chopin was born just outside Warsaw on February 22, 1810. For some reason, they officially list his birth date as March 1. Chopin's father was French, and his mother was Polish. His father, although being French, loved Poland and all things Polish and raised Frederic accordingly.

Chopin's parents were very musical and they taught him the piano at a very early age and it took off. Chopin was so gifted that he began giving concerts at age seven and had his first music published at age eight! Chopin was soon known throughout Europe as a young virtuoso, which means a highly accomplished musician. His music was mostly piano solos. He wrote and played many things including mazurkas and polonaises (dances) waltzes, nocturnes, and concertos.

This was the Romantic era. It was also a time when Poland did not have a country, so Chopin's music reflected this in his music, which stood for Polish nationalism. To escape the hostile conditions of Poland at the time, Chopin, at age twenty-one, did as so many Polish exiles did and escaped to Paris.

Paris in 1831 was the intellectual and artistic capital of the world, so Chopin, a genius without equal, fit in very well. He was friends with all the famous artists and writers living in Paris at the time. He didn't marry, but he had a long love affair with a writer named George Sand, a woman with a very boy-sounding name.

Chopin rarely performed in public. Once a year, he would give a concert at a place in Paris called Salle Pleyel. Chopin gave private piano concerts in his apartment where many of his works were first heard. Chopin died of tuberculosis in 1849 at age thirty-nine. He was buried in Pere Lachaise in Paris, France, but he had his heart cut out and sent back to Warsaw, Poland, where it's interred at the Church of the Holy Cross. Over 230 Chopin music works survive today.

On the west side of Detroit, there is a street named Chopin. It is right in the middle of the west side Polish neighborhood. My mother was born and raised on Chopin, and I also lived on Chopin when I was younger. The funny thing is that they call Chopin, cho-pin, the way it's spelled, rather than, show-pan, the way Frederic Chopin, Poland, and the entire classical world pronounces it. Nobody knows why, maybe because Chopin kind of rhymes with bowling pin.

Another person whose heart is interned at the Church of the Holy Cross in Warsaw is Wladyslaw Reymont, not a musician but worth mentioning. Wladyslaw Reymont was a famous writer who won the Nobel Prize for literature in 1924. Among Reymont's many works was Bunt, a story he wrote in 1922. Bunt is a story that describes a revolt by farm animals that take over a farm. It was a metaphor for the Bolshevik Revolution in Russia in 1917. If you think this sounds a lot like George Orwell's *Animal Farm*, I agree. Only Reymont's story was written twenty-three years earlier.

# HIGH SCHOOL

IN THE EIGHTH GRADE, ALL Catholic school students must take a test to see which Catholic high school they can get in to. The better your score, the better your school. Most of the Saint Suzanne boys picked Detroit Cathedral Downtown on Woodward, and most of the girls chose Rosary on Greenfield. I picked Salesian also on Woodward.

It looked like a good pick; an all-boys Catholic school downtown that looked to have a Polish connection. Salesian is an area of Poland, and the school colors were red and white—Polish colors. How could you get any more Polish than that?

But Salesian proved to be a little too unwise for me. I had to get up at five in the morning and ride three buses to school. We were required to wear a tie and coat every day. If we screwed up, we had to go to school on *Saturday*! And worst of all, they had this four-hundred-pound priest that I'll call Father Killer, beating the crap out of anyone who stepped out of line.

We had a drafting class right after lunch, and Father Killer was our teacher. We had a kid in the class who had a small speech impediment and had trouble pronouncing his name correctly. Father Killer would start the class by calling the young man up and asking him to say his name. He would stand up and say his name in his funny way.

"No, that's not correct. Now say it how you're supposed to!"

The scared student would then say his name again as best he could but incorrect. Father Killer would calmly get up from his front desk, stroll over to the poor guy as he rolled up his sleeves, grab him by his tie, and slap him two or three times across his face, and these were not love taps. Father Killer would then turn to the class and say, "Okay, boys, open up your books to page thirty-two."

I can think of a thousand things wrong with that scenario. Soon, Salesian and I parted ways amicably, and I was off to that huge west side temple of learning and mayhem, Cody High School, or as we liked to say, Detroit's best high school on Cathedral Street.

Cody wasn't a high school in the usual sense. It was a two-story holding tank, holding around four thousand west side teenagers for four or five hours every weekday. And I say four hours because that was it. At Cody, students came and went by shifts, some started at eight in the morning and were done by noon (first through fifth hours). Others started at noon and were done at 4:00 p.m. (sixth through tenth) and all hours in between. All day long, kids came and went, and nobody kept track.

On my first day at Cody, a teacher gave us a writing assignment for homework. I raised my hand and asked the teacher, "Does it have to be written in a certain color of ink?" At Salesian, all papers must be written in dark-blue ink. Anything else, and you would get a zero. "I don't care if you write the darn thing in crayon!" She laughingly answered. I knew then that I found a school where I would do okay.

Cody might not have been the best school in America, but it was a school that had every feature a modern school could offer as did most Detroit public schools back then. We had fully equipped shops and home economics classrooms, a four-hour trade drafting class, an auditorium, and cafeteria. We had a gym with an overhead running track, and a pool where we swam naked! Yes, we swam completely naked. Only the boys did. The girls wore bathing suits. How weird is that? I know but that's the way it was.

I can't recall ever learning anything at Cody but learning wasn't the real point of schools like Cody. It wasn't necessary. We were programmed to be factory workers at Ford or GM. We already knew how to read and write, do some math, and who George Washington and Hitler were. What more was there to learn? The factories were going strong in those days and paid well and that's the direction we were headed with the exception of a two-year Asian vacation.

The Vietnam war was raging, and we were all expected to do our part. "Do you want to stop the commies in Vietnam or on the Mississippi? Because they're coming." The teachers would tell us stuff like that whenever we complained about the draft. It seemed every year, we would learn of another Cody student who got killed in Nam. It was scary stuff hanging over our young heads.

Kids smoked back then. It's hard to imagine today fourteen-year-old kids stepping outside school and lighting up a cigarette but that's the way it was. Kools were the cigarette of choice. The ground outside Cody was covered in cigarette butts.

Cathedral Street was a boulevard, and outside were the grassy islands that make up the boulevard. The islands would be packed with kids skipping class and hanging out. Depending on who you hung with would be the direction you headed. Skipping class at Cody was always a two-day skip. The first day, the teacher would send a note to the counselor. The next day, the counselor's aid would come and hand the same note to the skipped student to be taken to the counselor's office. That note would then get tossed in the trash as the student headed back out to the island. No need to get yelled at by a counselor.

The islands were fun places. There was always something going on: laughing, crying, fighting, and cars peeling out. One day, we got a real surprise. Somebody put a bunch of old tombstones on the islands; nobody knew how they got there. Then the media found out and went ballistic. "Tombstones in front of Cody High School" was the big story!

Where the heck did they come from? We all wondered. It didn't take the cops very long to figure it out. It seemed a bunch of kids from the neighborhood were at a lake and stumbled across an old Civil War era cemetery. They ended up digging up some of the old coffins (yikes, grave robbers) and removing the tombstones and putting them on the islands in front of Cody. The crazy world of Cody.

One block south of Cody on Joy Road were a couple of cool places. The Cookie Queen had pop and doughnuts and booths where we could sit and hang out all day long. They never threw us out. A couple of blocks down Joy was A&G, the best hamburgers and fries in the city. Farther down Joy on the corner of Evergreen sat a little white hamburger stand called Jan's. A gang of teenagers hung out there sometimes called the BS Boys. A mile down Evergreen on the corner of Warren Avenue was another hamburger stand called Randy's. Another group of teenagers sometimes called the Warendale Gang hung out there. Most of us stayed clear of those two places.

This was the sixties, and as they say, times were a changing. Cody was mostly blue-collar working class folks that change didn't sit well with. The hippie scene was starting, and the Cody kids were fighting it the best they could. Not many kids had long hair at Cody. One that did was a boy we called Ringo. He had longer hair and looked just like Ringo from the Beatles.

One day, Ringo, Gary, and I were walking down the halls between classes when three Cody football players stopped us.

The biggest one of the group grabbed Ringo and said, "Look at this punk. Let's give him a haircut!"

"At least he's not as ugly as you!" my friend Gary promptly retorted.

"What? Who said that?" the biggest of the three football players screamed. "I'll kick all three of your asses right now with one hand tied behind my back!"

At five foot two and 120 pounds soaking wet, I was the biggest of the three of us, and all three of them were over six feet tall and at least two hundred pounds. He kept screaming at us, and we just stood there trying to figure out some good way to get out of this jam, but we knew there wasn't any. By now, all hallway traffic had stopped, and they formed a big circle around us and amusingly watched the show as we were verbally squashed to even bigger nothings than we were just two minutes earlier. Then a teacher walked up and broke it up sending us all on our way.

But that's the way it was back then. It took a lot of courage to grow your hair long in the sixties. It even took a little courage to be friends with the long hairs, and they were some of the nicest kids in school. All over the city, long hairs were getting harassed, beat up, and sometimes killed, and not just at Cody. Cooley, Redford, just about all the white high schools had trouble. The one exception was

Cass Tech. That's where the smart kids went; they were a little more progressive.

Gary Lapalm was one of the nicest kids you ever wanted to meet. He was way ahead of his time, knew all the newest music, and there was so much great music coming out in the sixties. Gary also liked to read stuff like the Beat Generation. Gary always had a smile on his face, liked everybody, and talked to everybody. The kind of person who would make me smile whenever I ran into him. Gary was one of the first guys at Cody to grow his hair long down to his shoulders. He wore one of those leather coats with the fringes, like Wild Bill Cody wore, like the hippies wore. Gary was one of our first hippies.

There was a dance one September night in 1968. Gary didn't even go. At that dance, a leather coat was stolen, and somehow, Gary Lapalm got blamed for it, and the boys went looking for him. They found him walking by a school. Gary wasn't worried even though they were greasers and he was a hippie because he knew these guys from the neighborhood. He should have been. They jumped Gary and beat him up. Gary died the next morning.

The media reported the story as another longhaired kid beat up by greasers. It was happening all over the city. It was hard to be different. Then a few years later, everyone, including the greasers, had long hair and was listening to Led Zeppelin and the Stones. It was a wild time.

But that wasn't the biggest sensualized crime in our little part of the city. The biggest happened on the night of June 23, 1967. A bunch of kids from Warrendale were down in the park by the Whitehouse (an old white mansion left to the city by a Ford executive). They had a bonfire going and were drinking and joking around when two couples who happened to be black joined them; big mistake.

One of the black men was Danny Thomas, a twenty-seven-year-old Vietnam veteran who worked at Ford. The lady with him was his wife who was pregnant with their first child. Some type of a fight broke out, and Danny ended up getting shot and killed, and his wife later miscarried. The police arrested six of them and ended up releasing five and held one for trial. The trial took seventeen months, and later he was acquitted.

I could only imagine something like that happening in these times and what would follow. But following this incident exactly one month later was the Detroit Riot.

# WORLD WAR II

WORLD WAR II WAS THE greatest war in history. It was also America's greatest moment in history. America won the war while Americans were spared many of the horrors that other countries experienced. World War II was a pretty good deal for Americans, except, of course, the four hundred thousand Americans killed, but a pretty bad deal for Poland.

Poland only had her country back twenty years when it started. Every American knows the lead up to World War II. Hitler was a horrible person who wanted to rule the world and nobody stood up to him. But if someone did, World War II would never have happened. If I had a dollar every time I heard someone say this, I would be rich.

The person they talk about who didn't stand up to Hitler is Neville Chamberlin, the Prime Minister of Great Britain. Germany had secretly built up her military and wanted revenge for losing World War I. Hitler began enlarging Germany by annexing surrounding, weaker countries. England and France did not want war. Their people had just fought the Great War, twenty years earlier and were burned out. Who could blame them? England had lost seven hundred thousand soldiers, and France had lost over a million. Chamberlin must have known that avoiding war with Hitler would be better than going to war and losing, so he signed the Munich Accord, "Peace for our time," which gave a chunk of Czechoslovakia to Germany.

The next country in Hitler's crosshair was Poland. Poland controlled a piece of land called the Danzig corridor. That was land that gave Poland access to the Baltic Sea but cut through Germany. Hitler wanted it. Every country had given in to Hitler, but not Poland. Poland was the first country in the world to stand up to this madman.

Things kept getting worse. On August 23, Germany shocked the world by signing a pact with the world's other madman, Stalin, the leader of Russia. This was called the Molotov-Ribbentrop Pact. It made The Soviet Union and Nazi Germany partners. The next day, both England and France formed a pact with Poland. World War II was all set and just eight days away.

England told Poland all it had to do was hold out for two weeks. Yes, that's it. Two weeks, and the British and French armies would be in Poland kicking the Nazi's butt. Of course, this never happened, but it gave Poland more courage, liquid courage perhaps.

On the morning of September 1, 1939, World War II began. The day started with the Germans having a masquerade party. German soldiers dressed as Polish soldiers raided a German border guard station. Hitler told his people because of this border incident that he must retaliate; after all, German pride is at stake. The German people mostly agreed, and the German Army invaded.

Almost two million German troops invaded Poland that fateful day. The Germans had 2,600 tanks against Poland's 180 and over 2,000 modern aircraft against Poland's mostly outdated 420. By September 14, Warsaw was surrounded. Two days after the invasion, on September 3, both England and France, to Germany's surprise, declared war on Germany. But it did little good; no British or French troops would show up or ever show to help Poland. As always, Poland stood alone.

The Polish Army took a stand at Warsaw and fought bravely. Then on September 17, the Russians invaded Poland from the east with over a million troops. It was over. Poland surrendered on October 5, lasting twice as long as anyone expected. In that short time, the Polish Army managed to kill fifty thousand Germans, destroying almost seven hundred German planes and destroying close to one thousand German tanks and armored vehicles. Poland did more damage to the Germans with their small Army than the combined British and French armies would do the following year during the battle of France.

One thing I have to mention is that story we have all heard, usually from some idiot, about the Polish cavalry charging German tanks. Poland did have a cavalry with horses at the start of World War II just like most countries, including the United States, had. Poland planned to use their cavalry in a very unique way.

September is the rainy season in Poland, and most of the roads back then were dirt. Poland figured the German tanks would get stuck in the mud, so they equipped their cavalry solders with small portable anti-tank weapons. The plan was they would gallop up shoot and destroy the disabled tanks. Horses don't get stuck in the mud. But it didn't rain; it was one of the driest Septembers ever. I guess Mother Nature was pulling for the Nazis.

The Poles knew the Germans would attack in September because they broke the German secret code called an Enigma machine. The Germans used it for encryption and decryption of their secret war plans. In one of the greatest achievements of World War II, three Polish mathematicians led by Marian Rejewski broke the secret code. They gave this information to the British who used it to beat the Germans. The English have even made a couple of films about their clever code breakers breaking the German codes during the war. They seem to leave out a small part, that it was the Polish, not the English, who initially broke the secret German codes.

For six long years, Poland was occupied. Germans and the Russians both occupied Poland at first. Then Germany double-crossed Russia and attacked them, pushing them out of Poland all the way back to Moscow. Then the Russians turned the tide and beat the Germans and eventually retook Poland.

Six million Poles died during the war, and many cities, including Warsaw, were destroyed. Most of the Polish killed by the Germans died in extermination and concentration camps. Hitler hated the Polish almost as much as he hated the Jews and wanted to eliminate both races.

The Russians also weren't very fond of the Polish and took this time of occupation to also massacre the Polish. In a place called the Katyn Forest, the Russians massacred twenty-two thousand Polish: eight thousand of them were Polish Army officers, and the other fourteen thousand were Polish intellectuals like doctors, lawyers, professors, and other public servants. No country suffered more in World War II than Poland.

Poland fought back forming the largest underground Army in Europe called the Armia Krajowa or the NK for short. It consisted of 350,000 men and operated all over Europe. They spied for the Allies, blew up German trains and fuel dumps while saving many Jews.

On August 1, 1944, with the Russian Army on the banks of the Vistula River, the NK started the Warsaw Uprising. It was the largest home Army uprising of World War II. It lasted two months, and when it was over, two hundred thousand people died. The Germans completely leveled Warsaw. The Russians just sat there and watched the slaughter. They wouldn't even let Allied planes land at their airfields with supplies for the Polish. When it was over, and the Germans left, the Russians rolled in.

We often have seen films of the Americans and their tanks liberating Paris with the jubilant Parisians showering American soldiers with flowers. At that very same time, Russian tanks were rolling through what was left of Warsaw. I don't think the Polish were showering them with flowers.

When the war finally ended in 1945, Poland lost six million people, about a fifth of her population. Percentage-wise, no country sacrificed or suffered more. Germany, the country that started the war, lost seven million people; five million were soldiers. But Russia would win the numbers game with twenty-seven million killed, including eleven million soldiers. It's hard for me to have much sympathy for the Russians.

The irony of World War II was that it started when Germany invaded Poland. Then the war ended with Russia invading Poland and occupied her for the next thirty-five years. The same countries that encouraged Poland to stand up to Hitler stood by as the Russians took over Poland.

Today America and Poland are friends, and America wants to install missiles there. Russia is not happy about the missiles. If this should ever lead to war, I have to wonder if America will be any more loyal to Poland than all of her other friends throughout history were?

# Polish Fighter Pilots in the Battle of Britain

THE POLISH AIR FORCE FIGHTER pilots of World War II proved to be some of the best pilots in the world. When Germany invaded Poland in 1939, Germany had one of the most modern Air Forces in the world. The Polish Air Force consisted of old-fashioned, gull-winged monoplanes called P-7s and P-11s. Compared to Germany's modern Stuka and Messerschmitt fighter planes, Poland didn't stand a chance.

The German press reported that the entire Polish Air Force was destroyed on the ground in the first twenty-four hours, and the western presses as usual echoed every lying word. Truth is Poland hid their Air Force, and their pilots gave the Germans a hard time shooting down 126 German planes. Not bad for a destroyed Air Force.

When Poland surrendered, hundreds of pilots escaped to France and joined the French Air Force. Then when France surrendered, they crossed the Channel and joined the Royal Air Force, eventually forming the famous Kosciuszko Squadron.

At first, the English were not very interested in the Polish pilots. They couldn't speak English, which could be a problem listening to the English-speaking dispatchers. Plus the English believed the German propaganda that the whole Polish Air Force was destroyed in twenty-four hours. Who would want these guys? But the Brits were in a jam. They lost so many of their pilots, and they couldn't train new ones fast enough, so out of desperation, they agreed to let the Polish fly.

On August 31, 1940, RAF Squadron 303, the Kosciuszko Squadron, went operational. They were not given the newer Spitfire airplanes. Instead, they were given the slower, less effective Hurricanes. The Poles didn't care because these planes were a hundred times better than anything they had flown in Poland.

The Polish formed their own way of flying. They did not fly in tight formations like the English. Instead, they flew in loose formations so they could spend more time looking for Germans and less time looking at their wingman. They hated the Germans who were back in Poland killing their people, and they made them pay for it over the English skies. They would fly full speed straight into the Germans with guns blazing. It was a modern charge of the old Polish cavalry.

They were very effective. By September 31, in just one month, they had shot down one hundred German planes. By the end of the Battle of Britain, Poles had a six to one kill score versus the British who had a three to one kill score. All this while the Polish were flying the Hurricanes, and the British were flying the newer Spitfires. England eventually formed sixteen Polish fighter squadrons. By war's end, they were accredited with destroying 332 German aircraft.

At the end of the war, the Polish were treated by England the same as they had always been treated, badly! England held a big victory parade in London and invited everyone who helped her win except Poland. Despite all that the Poles had done for England and all the blood they had shed for her, they were kept out of the parade. Russia demanded that the Polish be kept out of the parade, or they wouldn't be in it. England capitulated.

When World War II ended, many of the Polish soldiers and pilots who fought for England wanted to stay in England. After all, they laid their lives on the line to defend England, they earned the right to stay. This is where it gets crazy. England said all the Polish soldiers had to go back to Poland. While the Russians ordered all the returning Polish soldiers to be arrested and sent to prison for treason. This became a big issue in England: what to do with the Polish. Some of the English wanted them to stay, and some wanted them out: "Hey, what are they staying for? To take our jobs? The war's over.

Get going." In the end, some got to stay, some had to go, and some even came to America.

Today in England, two English Lords, Michael Ashcroft and Norman Tebbit, are campaigning for a one-million-pound monument to be built in London's Hyde Park honoring the Polish pilots who flew with the RAF during World War II. Lord Tebbit said, "Without the Polish, we would have lost the Battle of Britain!" (Here! Here!)

Polish RAF pilots performed well fighting the Germans in World War II but how well did America's Polish pilots do? Pretty darn good. In fact, America's greatest ace in Europe was a Polish American named Francis "Gabby" Gabreski. Gabby shot down more German planes than any other American pilot in World War II.

Gabby was born in Oil City, Pennsylvania, to parents who immigrated from Poland and opened a store in Oil City. Gabby was a pretty good student who got into Notre Dame University but quit after a couple of years. War was breaking out, and Gabby wanted to fly. He joined the Army Air Corp and soon was flying.

Gabby followed the exploits of the Kosciuszko Squadron and requested to be sent to England to train and learn from the experienced Poles. The Air Force agreed and sent him to Europe where Gabby flew twenty combat missions with the 303. They must have taught him well.

When America got into the war, Gabby was assigned to the Fifty-Sixth Operations Group of the Air Force. Flying the P47 Thunderbolt (not the quicker P51 Mustang), Gabby shot down twenty-eight German planes, two more than Eddie Rickenbacker, our greatest World War I ace.

On July 20, 1944, while strafing some German-parked planes in Russecheim, Germany, Gabby's prop hit the runway (that's flying pretty low), and he crashed. He was captured by the Germans and spent the rest of the war as a prisoner in Stalag Luft I.

After the war, they sent Gabby to Detroit, of all places, to be in charge of his old unit, the Fifty-Sixth Operations Group at Selfridge Air Force Base. They were now flying the brand-new F86 Sabre Jets.

When the Korean War broke out, the Air Force sent Gabby and the Fifty-Sixth Operations Group to Korea where he became an ace for the second time. Gabby shot down six and a half North Korean Migs for a total of thirty-four and a half kills.

When Gabby returned to the United States after the war, San Francisco gave him a ticker tape parade, and the key to the city. That was great, but I wonder why I have never heard of our American hero Gabby before researching this book?

# EDDIE SLOVIK

EDDIE SLOVIK WAS KNOWN AS the unluckiest man in the world. He was the only American soldier shot for desertion during World War II. Not surprising to some, Eddie was a Polish boy from the City of Detroit.

Eddie was born in Detroit on February 18, 1920, to Anna and Joseph Slowikowski. Eddie grew up to be a petty thief in and out of reform schools and later jails. Eddie usually got caught for everything he did.

When the war broke out, because of his criminal record, Eddie was given a 4F unfit for duty classification. Eddie thought he wouldn't have to go into the Army and was okay with that.

Eddie got a job as a laborer at a plumbing company in Dearborn where he met his wife, a bookkeeper named Antoinette Wisniewski. Eddie and Antoinette married on November 7, 1942. Soon after that, Eddie got a better job at the Desoto plant on McGraw and Wyoming where a ton of Polish Detroiters, including yours truly, worked. Eddie and his bride were able to move into their own place on the west side. This was Eddie's happiest time. Eddie thought that his luck had changed.

Just after Christmas 1943, Eddie received a letter from Uncle Sam. It was his draft notice. The war was cranking up, and the US needed more men, so they decided to lower the draft requirements to include 4Fs. Eddie knew that his bad luck was back. Eddie left Detroit for Texas for basic training on January 24, 1944. He would be dead in little over a year.

Eddie was a decent-enough soldier. He finished basic training and infantry school and then he received orders to Europe. Eddie sent his wife, Antoinette, 376 letters during his 372 days as a soldier.

Eddie arrived in France on August 20, 1944. He was assigned to the Twenty-Eighth Infantry Division US Army. In his first battle, Eddie was separated from his unit and ended up with a group of Canadian soldiers whom he stayed with for the next month. This was a pretty common occurrence during the war, so Eddie didn't get into any trouble. When he finally was reunited with his American unit, Eddie handed them a note he had written saying that he was a deserter, and he would not fight.

Eddie's commanding officer tried to talk him out of it. "Come on, Eddy, just rip up this letter. Go back to your unit, and we'll forget all about it," he said.

They gave him every opportunity to change his mind. They even offered to send him to another unit. But Eddie refused. Eddie was a coward who wouldn't fight. Eddie figured that he would get sent to prison, something he was very used to and could easily handle. As far as getting out with a dishonorable discharge, So what, he already had a record.

But Eddie's timing was bad. America was in the middle of a ferocious battle with the Germans, The Battle of the Bulge. Soldiers were getting killed and wounded by the thousands plus many were deserting or inflicting self-wounds trying to get out of combat. It was so bad that groups of deserters were robbing Army supply trucks and selling the stolen stuff on the black market. Something had to be done. The Army needed to make an example.

Eddie was tried in a military tribunal by a group of noncombat officers. The military usually uses noncombat officers when trying deserters because combat officers who have actually been in battle are usually more sympathetic to the deserters. I'd say that's also true in life.

To Eddie's surprise, he was sentenced to death by a firing squad. Eddie's appeals were no good. He even wrote a letter to General Eisenhower asking for mercy. Ike turned him down. Ironically,

General Eisenhower, a five-star general and commander of all Allied Forces had personally never been in combat.

Eddie was sentenced to die on January 31, 1945. They picked a French chateau with a high-masonry wall for his execution. They didn't want the French civilians to know what was happening. Twelve soldiers with good marksmanship were selected from the Twenty-Eighth Infantry Division, Eddie's old division. Eleven soldiers would be firing a live round with one firing a blank. Eddie was tied to a makeshift pole in the courtyard.

The priest who escorted Eddie out said, "Eddie, when you get up there. Say a prayer for me."

"Okay, Father. I'll pray that you don't follow me too soon." That would be Eddie's last words.

All eleven shots fired at Eddie hit their target, but he was still alive. "Can't you guys shoot straight?" Was reportedly what the examining doctor shouted as he examined Eddie. Eddie died as the firing squad was reloading for another volley. Eddie was buried at a small cemetery in France with ninety-five other executed American soldiers who were all there for high crimes such as murder and rape. Eddie was the only deserter.

Fifty thousand Americans deserted during World War II. Of the fifty thousand deserters, twenty-one thousand were tried for desertion. Of the twenty-one thousand tried, forty-nine were sentenced to death. And of the forty-nine sentenced to death, forty-eight were commuted, and one was carried out. They didn't call Eddie unlucky for nothing.

It's funny because they executed Eddie because the Battle of the Bulge was going badly, but the battle was over and America had won before the execution was carried out. Also, they said that they wanted to set an example, but they Kept Eddie's execution secret. It wasn't until 1954 when the excellent book, *The Execution of Private Slovik*, written by William Bernard Huie came out that Americans soldiers or civilians found out.

In 1960, Frank Sinatra wanted to make a movie about Eddie Slovik, but he received a lot of flak from people including Joe Kennedy, President John Kennedy's father.

Then in 1974, a made-for-TV movie, *The Execution of Private Slovik*, based on Huie's book, came out starring Martin Sheen. It was a big hit; the number one made-for-TV movie. The timing was right. The Vietnam war, where fifty-eight thousand Americans died, had just ended, and the draft that touched millions of families in America had also just ended. Americans had empathy for Eddie. I don't believe a film about an Army deserter would be that popular today.

In 1987, a Macomb County Commissioner named Bernard V. Calka, a Polish American and a World War II veteran, raised five thousand dollars and had Eddie's remains brought back to America. He was buried at Woodmere Cemetery next to wife, Antoinette. Eddie is finally back where he wanted to be. Not everyone can be a hero.

# American Polish in World War II

WELL, THEY SHOT EDDIE SLOVIK, but he was in no way indicative of the rest of us Polish people. One million Polish Americans joined the armed services during World War II. That is one million out of five million Poles living in America at the time: one out of five.

It would be hard for any other ethnic group in America to match that. Polish made up just 4 percent of the American population during World War II but made up 8 percent of the armed services. Yes, we are loyal and proud Americans who do not shirk our duty.

The morning of December 7, 1941, my mom's twin brother, Uncle Hank, was awoken by a loud bang. He ran to his barracks window and saw the USS Arizona blown up and hundreds of Japanese planes flying overhead. He was at Pearl Harbor waiting for his ship to get fixed. My mom and her mother and sisters didn't know if Uncle Hank was dead or alive for two weeks. Then a postcard from the Navy arrived with one line, "Your son, Henry Slawek, is alive and well." Welcome to World War II!

My father and his four brothers all joined the Army. Two of them went to the Far East, and one fought in The Battle of The Bulge with General Patton. My dad was sent home. My dad was the brainiac of the family. He went to Cass Tech back when it was the finest high school in America and then to Lawrence Tech to study engineering. He was working at General Motors in an engineering department. The Army needed him to stay at GM.

General Motors, along with Ford and Chrysler, stopped all auto production and began making armaments for the military. My father worked at General Motors Research Laboratory, which was the Argonaut Building, the big red building behind GM Headquarters. The building was surrounded by armed guards and all kinds of top-secret work was going on inside.

General Motors had just gotten the contracts to help design and build the weapons that the military needed including the Boeing B-29 Superfortress Bomber, the most expensive project of World War II. Most people think the Manhattan Project (atom bomb) was the most expensive project of World War II. Nope, it was the B-29.

A huge part of the war effort happened right here in Detroit. The Arsenal of Democracy was where thousands of Polish people worked making the products that brought America victory.

The Polish women of Detroit went to work too. My mom worked at Cadillac on Clark Street where they made the M5 tanks. My aunt Cassie worked at the Willow Run Aircraft Factory where they built the Consolidated B-24 Liberator. That was also the plant where Rose Will Monroe, better known as Rosie the Riveter, worked.

Rose Will Monroe was one of the millions of women who entered the work place for the first time during World War II. As the men marched off to war, the women took their places at the factories. They were badly needed as the factories switched from peacetime goods to wartime armaments. They made a poster of Rosie wearing a bandana and her sleeves rolled up saying, "We can do it!" And do it they did. Thousands of Detroit women; many were Polish.

When Henry Ford first got the contract to build the B-24, the government hoped that he could build one B-24 bomber a day. Ford told them he could build one an hour. It was unheard of to build aircraft that fast, but Ford did it. That was Detroit's story in World War II. We built everything: planes, tanks, bombs, machine guns, and jeeps to name a few. They were faster and better than just about anywhere else in the world. Without Detroit, they couldn't win that war. We were the Arsenal of Democracy!

They sent my uncle Eugene and uncle Wesley to the Far East to fight. They sent my uncle Edmond to Europe where he fought with Patton in The Battle of the Bulge.

As a kid growing up in the 50s and 60s, family gatherings were filled with uncles and aunts telling us wartime stories. The TV show, *Twentieth Century*, with all the World War II films was never missed. I can still hear their voices as we watched. "Oh yeah. I remember that," or "Hey, I think that was my outfit!" World War II was an honored moment for all Americans, and a proud moment for Polish Americans who did so much. What a great time in history.

Years later, as he was close to death, my uncle Edmond, who wasn't married, called me over to help settle his affairs. We spent a long time talking over war stories, and I enjoyed every one. Uncle Edmond was in the thick of things and brought back a few mementoes. He gave me a German Mauser pistol that he took off a Nazi General whom he captured plus a bayonet and a few Nazi medallions. I will always cherish this stuff. I know the sacrifice he made to get them. My uncle Edmond, like so many other Polish Americans, was a true American hero.

One of my earliest memories was going to Willow Run Airport to send off my cousin David to the Army. He came back twenty-five years later, a major with three tours of Vietnam under his belt.

Growing up with the Vietnam War and the draft was pretty heavy for us young boys. It seems half the boys from Cody got drafted and sent to Nam, and more than a few never returned. I had three cousins my age, Richard, Tommy, and Dennis, who all got drafted and sent to Vietnam. All three returned. Thank goodness. As far as myself, somehow I managed to get into the Navy Reserves. The closest I got to Vietnam was San Diego where the weather was beautiful, the chow was fantastic, and not a Vietcong for thousands of miles.

# Racing in the Street

THE DREAM OF EVERY BOY growing up in Detroit in the late sixties was a cool car. We were the Motor City, and Detroit was making the coolest and fastest cars in the world. We all wanted one. Every fall, the new cars would come out; new styles, new colors, and more horsepower. The Beach Boys and other groups sang about Detroit cars and street racing. Cars were big everywhere in America but no bigger than in the City of Detroit.

I worked every part-time job the neighborhood offered but at none of them would I earn enough for a cool set of wheels. One day I saw an ad in the Redford Courier looking for workers at some sort of modernization company. I called and got a job as a door-to-door canvasser, and I soon became the Tiger Woods of door-to-door canvassers.

The city was changing. Neighborhoods were going from all white to all black overnight. Our company's unique idea was to approach these new home owners and find what home improvements they needed, and we did it all from roofs to carpeting to remodeled basements. If they asked if we made lemon pies, we said, "With or without meringue, ma'am?"

Many of the neighborhoods we canvased door to door were in high-crime areas, and some of the new guys were afraid to get out of the car, but not me. There was a popular DJ on WCHB, a black radio station back then who called himself Robby D. So I called myself Bobby D. I think some of the folks thought I was the DJ. We sold tons of stuff, and I made tons of money. Soon I had enough to buy my dream car, a brand-new 1968 Pontiac GTO!

It was the days of street racing and cruising drive-ins. It was a great time to have a nice ride. The drive-in in our neighborhood was Daley's on Plymouth and Burt; an okay place but not what I would call a hot-rod drive-in. Instead of cool fast cars, Daley's was usually filled with VWs, MGs, and kids in their parents' cars, Ford Falcons with a Kleenex box on the dashboard. And the kids that hung up there usually headed home early to do their homework. I think they were planning to go to college or something. I needed a little more action.

Soon I found myself on Warren Avenue where all the Polish kids lived. Cars meant a lot more to this crowd. Everyone had one, or they were working toward getting one. Nobody here talked of college. The future for them would be in the factory and usually the same one their dad worked at. They lived in aluminum-sided one-story-and-a-half bungalows with manicured lawns and a one-car garage in the back where their old man kept his three-year-old four-door Chevy or Plymouth. Out front parked in the street would be the kids' spotless brand-new SS 396 or Olds 442 or a Ford GT 390.

The streets and drive-ins would be screaming with excitement with music blasting, tires screeching, girls laughing, and everybody having fun. The fun would go on until late at night. Who cared about working or going to school tomorrow? Most of the kids on Warren were blue-collar kids who lived for the moment. They knew these were their best days. One year from now, half of them would be thousands of miles away sloshing through a rice paddy while carrying a M16. Their shiny Plymouth GTX would still be parked in front of their parents' house but with a for-sale sign. Their parents hoped they could sell it before they would have to pick up the payments.

Everyone was a Democrat back then just like their parents. Today when I run into those guys from the old neighborhood, they often have a red cap covering their graying head with Make America Great Again. They live in places like Canton or Brighton and never go back to the old neighborhood. A few of them still have a nice cruiser in their garage, and on Wednesday evenings, they head to a local parking lot meet up with other cruisers and reminisce of old times. They just don't stay out very late.

West Warren had three drive-ins: A&W which we all called A&Dobja's (it was in the Polish neighborhood), Dailey's down by the park, and Little Skippers just past the park. The lots would be full of cars, GTOs, 442s and Road Runners all backed in. We never pulled forward into our spot. We backed in. We'd hang out for an hour or so, maybe get a burger and a Coke and then head west on Warren to Telegraph.

Telegraph was the mother load of West Side Detroit street racing. From Eight Mile to Northline, there were fifteen straight miles of beautiful asphalt with traffic lights spaced exactly one mile apart. Thousands of kids cruising in hot cars, windows down, radio blasting, and all looking for a race. I could shut my eyes and know exactly when the light turned green by the instant sounds of engines roaring and tires squealing. There they go! The strip went through five different cities and five different police departments. I think every one of those cops knew me by my first name.

Late on Friday and Saturday nights, we would make a right turn on Northline and drive to where it dead-ends where there would be hundreds of cars lined up to race. They even had starters waving checkered flags. Racing would go on until two or three in the morning, and I'd be there until the end. My Goat (GTO) was pretty fast. I'd shut them down and shut them up. For some reason, the cops usually left us alone on Northline.

On Sundays, we would drive a little farther down Telegraph to Sibley, make a left turn, and on the corner of Dix stood the temple of drag racing, Detroit Dragway. For a few bucks, we got to race legally. They would put you in a class and mark it on your window. Winners would get a trophy. After us little guys raced, the big names would come out. Detroit legends: The Ramchargers, Bob Ford Thunderbolt, Royal Pontiac GTO, and my favorite, Seaton's Shaker! When it was over, we'd head back to A&Dobja's for a pop and a burger, then some more cruising down Telegraph.

*Cause summer's here, and the time*
*is right for racing in the street!*

—Bruce Springsteen

93

# CELEBRATED DAYS IN POLAND

JUNE 22, SUMMER SOLSTICE, IS a celebrated day in Poland. It is also called Saint John the Baptist Day. Another name for June 22 is Kupala Night. It is the first day of summer, the longest day and shortest night of the year. The celebration of this day goes back to pagan times when people celebrated the summer solstice. After the pagans converted to Christianity, the Church changed the name of the holiday to Saint John's Day.

Kupala Night or Saint John's Day, whichever, is a pretty wild night in Poland. Young people go into the woods after dark and build fires, then jump over them. Young men would jump over the fire to show off their virility. Couples also would jump over the fire while holding hands to see if they should be together. If they make it over, yes, they should be together. Not making it over seemed like a hard way to discover she or he's not the one. The Kupala fires also represent the pagan custom of sacrifice.

Girls wear white dresses and flower wreaths on their heads. They throw the wreaths into the river and wait to see which lucky boy finds it. The girls or maidens then make a circle around the fire and sing erotic songs and dance erotic dances. Eating eggs and drinking liquor is customary. Then they couple up and go into the woods looking for magic ferns that bloom. It is believed that on this night deep in the woods, some ferns bloom. I don't know if any fern ever actually bloomed, but other blooming was happening. Kupala Night is the only night that free love is okay in Poland. It is interesting that the Polish did not bring the Kupala celebration to America. Perhaps they didn't want to offend the Puritans.

Our grandparents and their grandparents plus years and years of forgotten ancestors celebrated Kupala Night back in Poland. Kupala is in our Slavic blood. That's probably why as a teenager, we would go down to Rouge Park on summer nights and make fires and then jump over them like our ancestors did. I just wish I would have known about those blooming ferns.

The Monday after Easter is a holiday in Poland called Dyngus day. On Dyngus day, boys chase girls with sticks or pussy willows and whack their back ends. Palms were hard to get in Poland, so on Palm Sunday, they passed out pussy willows instead of palms. Palms were looked at as sacred charms that protect homes from lightning and other bad things.

Dyngus day goes back to pagan times and is linked to the goddess of fertility. It's a tough day for girls. It starts with buckets of water thrown on them at daybreak while they are still sleeping. Sometimes they are dragged out of bed and thrown into the river. A good-looking girl can expect to get soaked many times on Dyngus day. Girls offer boys painted eggs not to get them wet. On Tuesday, it's the girl's turn to throw water on the boys.

March 21. The equinox or the first day of spring is called Marzanna day to celebrate the end of winter and beginning of spring. Marzanna was a Slavic goddess back in pagan times.

Children walked down to the river and threw a little doll or Marzanna made of straw and dressed in traditional clothes into the river. They never looked back because it was bad luck. If they didn't live by a river, then they burned an effigy of Marzanna. They did this to be sure winter was over.

In the 1800s, the Catholic Church tried to stop this old Slavic custom and replaced it with throwing an effigy of Judas from church towers on Easter Wednesday, but people liked the old Marzanna effigy better, and it still continues to this day in Poland.

# ALL SAINTS' DAY

ONE GREAT THING ABOUT GOING to a Catholic school was that we always got the day after Halloween off. After trick or treating all night long, our public school friends had to get up the next morning and go to school, but not us Catholics. It was All Saints' Day, a Catholic holiday. We would get together with our classmates and compare our bags of candy, and then trade. I would trade whatever they wanted for their Butterfinger and Babe Ruth candy bars, which were my favorite.

Lost in all this bluster was why we had the day off. We seldom went to church on All Saints' Day although the nuns told us that we had to, because it was a holy day of obligation. And we didn't go to cemeteries to visit our dead relatives. In fact to this very day few people in America go to church on All Saints' Day, although the night before "All Hallows Eve" has become one of America's biggest holidays.

Compare that to Poland where they have no idea what trick or treating on Halloween is, but they all celebrate All Saints' Day. It is an official holiday in Poland and at least 16 other European Catholic countries. All offices, schools and government buildings are closed on All Saints' Day.

Next to Christmas and Easter, All Saints' Day is the biggest holiday in Poland and probably the most sacred. Nobody celebrates All Saints' Day like the Polish. People return from far away to clean and polish their relatives' headstones. Polish headstones are big and fancy, and no two are the same. The one exception is that they all have a stone cross.

96

The evening starts at home with a huge Polish meal. After the meal, the leftover food is wrapped up and taken to the cemetery, where they eat again in a celebration with their dead ancestors. People also bring candles and seasonal flowers to decorate all the graves. It is really something to see every grave lit up by candles and covered with flowers, a sea of flowers overlapped by a sea of light. Even the most forgotten graves are also decorated.

Monuments to famous Poles and Polish soldiers graves are decorated. The Army sends out soldiers to stand guard at the graves of the many soldiers and freedom fighters killed in all the wars and uprisings of the past.

Beggars come to the cemeteries and ask for food. They are looked at differently in Poland. Like in America, many of their beggars or homeless have mental issues. Polish people often think these touched people have a way to communicate with dead spirits, so they are treated with respect and are often offered to join in with the meal and festivities. This is in hopes that they will communicate and send good tidings to their loved ones.

All Saints' Day goes back to old pagan times where on November 1, most things in nature either died or went dormant. Back then, people gathered and called up souls and discussed their lifelong deeds according to old folk wisdom. People were judged not only by what they did do but also by what they didn't do. Cruelty, greed, and pride were considered mortal sins.

On November 2, Polish people return to the cemeteries and pray for all the souls in purgatory so that they may enter the kingdom of heaven.

# Detroit Goes Hippie

WHEN I RETURNED TO DETROIT after my stint in the Navy Reserves, I found that the town had changed. All my good greaser buddies got married, sold their hot rods, and settled down. The drive-ins were thinning out. Not a whole lot of people drag raced on Telegraph anymore. They even stopped playing the Sunday at Detroit Dragway commercials on the radio. Radio changed too. WKNR Keener 13 on the AM dial was out, and WABX the Air Aces on the FM dial was so in.

I would stop by a friend's apartment, and after an hour or two of watching black-and-white TV, while getting the bad eye from his wife, I'd be ready to leave. The times were changing. I needed a new scene, and I sure found one.

I ran into my old high school friend, Gary Brocket. We went for a ride in his 65 GTO. He pulled out a joint and said, "You smoke pot?"

"Sure," I lied.

Next thing I knew, we were over somebody's house on Tiremen. They were four younger kids who I think were still in Cody High School. They were sitting around their parents' living room listening to one of those stereos with the big speakers that were so popular back then. I was stoned out of my mind, and suddenly, Jimi Hendrix's "Stone Free" came blasting out of those big speakers. We might not remember the sixties, but we can remember that first song we heard stoned. I can still hear that cowbell. "Turn me loose, baby."

That was it for me. I was into a new world. Music became our thing, replacing cars. Soon my GTO was gone, and I was driving a yellow VW Beatle. The Time restaurant on Plymouth and Braile became my new hangout. A patty melt, fries and milk half white, and half chocolate was my standard order. My nice shirts and pants and leather shoes were replaced with Levis, Converse All Stars, and T-shirts, except for winter where I would add a flannel shirt to my attire. Barbershops became a thing of the past.

Sitting at the counter at the Time Restaurant, finishing my patty melt, I heard someone say, "Man, look at you!" I turned, and there was a longhaired freak that I knew from school named Rich. "Look at *you*!" I said and the next thing I knew we were good friends hanging out together. It seemed that he knew everyone and everything that was happening and he introduced me to all of it.

They say decades start in their third year, so the 60s started in 1963 and ended in 1973. That was the great music decade, and few places on Earth had more music than Detroit. From Motown to the garage bands, Detroit was a happening place. Every group from the USA or England knew Detroit was a happening place and wanted to play here. I saw all of them, sometimes sitting in the front row.

I saw the Moody Blues at Cobo, Rod Stewart at the Eastown, J Geils at the Cinderella Ballroom the same night that they recorded their live album, *Full House*, T Rex at U of D, John Lennon at the Crisler for the John Sinclair Freedom Rally (tickets only cost two dollars), the MC5 at the Grande Ballroom were many groups like The Who and Cream made their USA debut, The Rolling Stones at the Masonic Temple, and Chicago at Pine Knob, where driving home was a pain in the butt for people heading south, and everybody headed south.

Plus there were free concerts all over Detroit in Rouge Park, Bell Isle, and Wayne State. Ann Arbor had all kinds of crazy stuff going on back then from free concerts to the annual hash bash. Ann Arbor was an American hippie capital, home of the SDS (Students for a Democratic Society). Ann Arbor hippie radicals would walk around dressed in green Army fatigues, kind of a radical Fidel Castro look. Today I see older white guys dressed in camo, a lot different than the old Ann Arbor hippies.

Al's bar on Joy Road and Evergreen became a cool place to go, and it all started on January 1, 1972, New Year's Day. That was the day the drinking age in Michigan was lowered to 18. We used to stop in Al's for a beer; the place would usually be empty. When we stopped in that night on our way back from a New Year's Eve party, we couldn't believe our eyes. Al's was packed; standing room only. Every eighteen-, nineteen-, and twenty-year-old in the neighborhood were there and then they came back night after night. Soon everyone called it Al's armed bar because of all the fights. It became the craziest bar on the West Side until they finally shut it down.

The Time restaurant where we all hung out was also the place all the cops from the sixteenth. Precinct drank their coffee and ate their chow. The counter would be lined with clean-cut, well-groomed policemen dressed in their starched light-blue shirts. Sitting across from them in the booths would be every weird, longhaired, half-buzzed miscreant the neighborhood possessed. The jukebox would be playing, people talking, laughing and eating, and everyone getting along. It was a beautiful thing.

A bunch of us got jobs at Chrysler Export Import on Burt Road. We would work six days a week and ten hours a day for a month and then they would lay us off for a month. We would pick up our unemployment checks, jump on I-75 south to sunny Florida where we had a ton of free places to stay. We would lay on the beach all day spending our unemployment checks on beer, weed, and suntan oil in that order. We became hippie beach bums, and life was a blast.

Then one day, I stopped by my parents' house, and my mom said, "Hey, Bob. You got a message from the Detroit Fire Department." I knew then and there that my hippie days had come to an end. I would soon be trading the long hair, bell-bottoms, and crazy shenanigans of my wild hippie youth for the red trucks, blue uniforms, and dangerous but interesting life of a Detroit fireman. Adulthood was knocking.

Legs Inn. Famous Polish restaurant in Northern Michigan.

St. Suzanne's School and Church. Where we raised Holy hell.

My house, 20612 Orangelawn, Detroit Home Sweet Home.

Rouge Pools. Our summertime hangout.

Cody High. The BEST High School on Cathedral.

Stan "The Man" Musial's jersey at the Polish-
American Sports Hall of Fame

American Polish Cultural Center in Detroit.

Kowalski's Famous kielbasa factory in Hamtramck, Michigan

The Author savoring a paczki at the New Palace
Bakery in Hamtramck, Michigan

New Palace Bakery in Hamtramck, Michigan.
Ground Zero on Paczki Day.

Sweetest Heart of Mary Church. Detroit's Polish Cathedral.

Dom Polski Hall on Junction Street, Detroit. Home
to thousands of Polish wedding celebrations.

St. Albertus. Detroit's first Polish Church.

Ladder 22. The Fire Station in Old Polonia that fed soup
to untold numbers during the Great Depression.

Old St. Casimer church. First Polish church on Detroit's
West Side. The original church was torn down and
replaced with this modern church in the 60's.

Dombrowski Field House at Orchard Lake St. Mary's Polish school.

Parents of the author at their wedding in 1946.

A canal in Gdansk, Poland. Home of Solidarity.

The author and his wife, Linda, at the top of the Warsaw Castle.

The Three Crosses. A monument to Solidarity at the Gdansk shipyard.

A street Auschwitz.

"Work Will Set You Free". Sign as you enter Auschwitz death camp.

The author and his mother on Orangelawn Street.

The author and his sisters, Nancy and Toni
decorating the family Christmas Tree.

The Markey Square in Kraków. The largest market square in Europe.

The Warsaw Castle. Stalin's gift to Poland.

Poster for The Polish Muslims playing a Paczki Day concert.

St. Stanislaus Kostka Church in St. Louis, Missouri.
Licensed under Creative Commons copyright.

Mermaid of Warsaw. Sculpture by Ludwika Nitschowa (1889-1989)
Licensed under Creative Commons copyrights.

# POLISH VODKA

THE WORD VODKA COMES FROM the Polish word meaning water. We can usually tell where something was invented by its name. Some people think Russia invented vodka, but there is no similar word for vodka in the Russian language. The word whiskey comes from the old classical Scott Gaelic word meaning water. So it's a pretty good guess that the Scottish people invented whiskey, or *whisky* as they spell it.

The first Polish vodka goes back to the middle ages, eleventh century, and was called gorzalka. It was primarily used for medicinal purposes. It would just be used for medicinal purposes for another four hundred years until 1400 when the Polish started drinking vodka for recreational purposes. The first recording of the word vodka was in 1405 at the Palatinate of Sandomierz, the government administration in Poland. It would be another hundred years before the word vodka would ever be recorded in Russia in 1533.

Polish grain vodka became very popular. By decree, everyone in Poland was free to make vodka and just about everyone did. In 1580, the city of Poznan alone had 498 distilleries producing vodka. For the next three hundred years, Polish vodka was exported all over Europe. A vodka belt developed in Europe consisting of Russia, Iceland, Norway, Sweden, Estonia, Latvia, and Lithuania with Poland right in the middle supplying all their thirsty neighbors with good Polish vodka.

But grain vodka was very expensive, so in the nineteenth century, Poland began making potato vodka, which brought the price of vodka way down. Also, Poland invented triple distilling, which greatly improved vodka, and in 1871, the Polish invented the first clear vodka: rectified spirit.

In the nineteenth century, Poland was divided in three and wiped off the map, but they still remained the world leader in vodka production. In 1836, there were 4,981 vodka distilleries in Galicia, and 2,094 vodka distilleries in the Russian sector. By this time, a lot of small Polish businessmen who were making vodka were doing very well. Then the royalty rescinded their decree letting everyone make vodka, and they took over all production of vodka. The rich got richer while the poor got drunk.

During the occupation of their country, the depressed Polish people drank a lot of vodka. The Russian Czar noticed the ill health of the Polish Army recruits and became alarmed. To slow down the drinking, he raised taxes on vodka and shortened the hours that taverns could be open.

Poland became free from the Czar and Russia in 1918 but that didn't last long. In 1945, when the Russians again took over Poland and made it a communist state, all vodka distilleries were taken over by the government. But that's not all. Russian propaganda tried to diminish Poland's role in inventing and developing vodka. This propaganda had worldwide implications as seen here in the USA where many people credit the Russians with inventing vodka.

Today in free Poland, there are many vodka distilleries producing the finest vodkas in the world. Chopin and Belvedere are a couple of very good but pricey Polish vodkas. Zabrowka vodka goes back to the sixteenth century and has a blade of bison grass in every bottle. Goldwasser vodka, which also goes back to the sixteenth century, has actual gold flakes in every bottle. Then there is Krupnik, a honey-flavored vodka and rectified spirit; a 192-proof vodka. Yikes! Sobieski and Lukosawa are two of my favorite vodkas and are both moderately priced.

So when you go into a store to buy a bottle of vodka, buy Polish. You won't regret it. It's the original.

# POLISH JOKES

HOW MANY POLISH DOES IT take to change a light bulb?

How can you tell who the groom is at a Polish wedding?

How do you sink a Polish battleship?

What's long and hard that a Polish woman gets on her wedding night?

I can go on and on, and I don't have to give you any of the punchlines because you've heard them all. Dumb Polish jokes.

Some loudmouth boor usually tells the jokes, and everyone laughs while looking at us. Then we wonder why do they make fun of us? What did we do or didn't do to become the butt of so many jokes. We have always been good Americans, obeying the laws, paying our taxes, fighting the wars, educating our children, cleaning our neighborhoods and working hard.

The jokes used to really hurt my father. Nobody loved this country more than him, and nobody was more upset by Polish jokes. Growing up in the fifties, sixties, and seventies, Polish jokes were all the rage, and as soon as someone found out my Polish name, out they came.

The media didn't help. A whole ton of TV shows made fun of Polish: *All in the Family*, *The Tonight Show*, *Rowan & Martin's Laugh-In* to name a few. It seemed we couldn't get a break. Who were the ones that started making fun of the Polish?

The answer is the Germans who are the ones history has accredited with starting the Polack jokes. They did it twice. First time was back around the turn of the century. Germans first arrived in America about fifty years before the Polish. They were well settled by the time the Polish arrived. The Polish came as refugees who were escaping oppression, and one of their main oppressors was the Germans.

Germany controlled a third of Poland and severely oppressed the Polish people. To sell this to the German people, the leaders often belittled the Polish. The German leaders, Frederick the Great and then Bismarck, both hated the Polish. They called them less than human. Germans were taught this, and many brought this thought to the new world.

When Americans in the land of the free started asking the Germans, "What's going on back in Europe? Why did you Germans take over Poland?" The Germans often answered that the Polacks are stupid and can't run their own country, and to prove this, they would often tell funny stories about the Polish. The new Polish refugees in their babushkas and ratty clothes who couldn't speak a word of English were in no position to defend themselves.

The second big push was in 1939; the start of World War II. Hitler and the Russians invaded Poland. Hitler and his propaganda ministers told the Americans and the world the same funny Polish stories that his German relatives had said forty years earlier. They had to invade Poland to save the incompetent bad Polish people from themselves. But this time, they had a friend—Hollywood! Hollywood didn't like Hitler, but many loved the Russian communist! And they did not want the commies to look like the bad guys for invading Poland, so they went along with the funny Polish stories. Stories that turned into Polish jokes: the Polish cavalry charging German tanks with spears.

I can recall as a kid growing up seeing two movies that featured Polish people. The first was *A Streetcar Named Desire* where Marlon Brando played the lead protagonist as a rude, crude, and dumb Pole who hung out at the bowling alley. The second was *Taras Bulba*, a film about the very good Russian Cossack's fighting their very bad Polish overlords. Hollywood made this movie in 1962 at the very height of the Cold War as Russian troops marched down the streets of Warsaw. It was also at the height of Polish jokes.

The days of the Polish jokes are not over. Drew Carey has made them on his show and so has Jimmy Kimmel. The *Polish plumber* is a derogatory term used in England where attacks against the Polish by right-wingers have doubled in the last couple of years.

The comedian Jackie Mason, the food critic Giles Coren, and former Senator Arlin Spector, who are all Jewish, can be seen on the net making derogatory remarks about us Polish. I watched their clips as I researched this book. At that time, I was reading an excellent book: *The Zookeeper's Wife* about a Polish Catholic who risked her and her family's life as she rescued many Jews from the Nazis in war-torn Poland.

But then they say, "Everyone gets made fun of: Italians, Irish, you name it!" No, not nearly the way us Polish have. For example, any comedian can get up on stage and say this: for all the Polish out there, I will speak slower, and get a laugh. Change the word Polish with any other nationality and will the same comedian get the same laughs? I don't think so.

Sometimes Polish people will tell Polish jokes, not me. I think it's wrong and not funny. I think us Polish should treat the Polish joke the same way blacks treat the N-word. And I also believe we shouldn't join in belittling other races or nationalities no matter how fashionable it may be. We, of all people, should know better. The Nazis didn't start by exterminating Jews, they started with crude jokes about Jews, and we all know how that ended.

# DETROIT FIREMAN

JUNE 26, 1972, I REPORTED to the Detroit Fire Department Training Academy to start my thirty-eight-year career as a Detroit firefighter.

After I graduated from the academy, they sent me to Engine 12 on West Warren and Lawton. Six months later, they sent me to Ladder 22 on McGraw and Martin right in the heart of the West Side Polonia. It was a brick two-story firehouse with an old worn-out Seagrave sixty-five-foot ladder truck parked inside. The crew was mainly senior firefighters riding out their time waiting to make sergeant. It was a rest camp, probably not the best place for a new firefighter.

The neighborhood was still very much as it had been for the last sixty years: street after street of well-maintained frame houses with big front porches. A bar or bakery was on every corner, and two big factories were on either side of McGraw, one at Livernois and the other one at Wyoming. Every six blocks was another Catholic Church with a Catholic school right next to it.

The folks living there were still predominantly Polish. Little old ladies in babushkas would push their wire carts to the market to shop for their daily meals. Men would stop at the bar after work for some conversation and a couple of boombas.

We hardly ever got any fires at Ladder 22. The area was pretty crime free. They still had the fireboxes on every corner. One evening, we got a box pulled run and when we pulled up, to our surprise, a good citizen was holding two kids, that looked around ten years old, he caught pulling the fire box. In my whole career, this was the only time this ever happened. We didn't know what to do with these two kids. Forget about those signs on fireboxes warning about hefty fines and jail time for people caught pulling false alarms. That never happened. The captain ended up yelling at them and then sent them home while the good citizen watched in confusion.

I soon found an upper flat on Chopin Street, the same street my mom grew up on. It was named after the great Polish composer, Chopin. Right about this time, the city changed the rule and let us firemen grow our hair long. Also around this time, the movie Serpico was out and a big hit. It was about a New York cop who grew his hair long and moved back into the city. That was me! I fixed my flat up the way I thought Serpico would. Yep, I was another Serpico. I would walk up to Michigan Avenue every day that I was off and do my shopping or go to the bar or get something to eat at the OK or the Starlight restaurant. I loved the neighborhood and could have lived there forever.

One of the bars I would stop in was Tip Top on Procter Street. It was the same bar my mother and father met in 1946. And it still looked the same.

I was starting to get bored running at Ladder 22, so I put in a transfer request asking for a busier fire company. They sent me two stations east to Ladder 4. This was a bigger firehouse with two fire trucks and a younger crew. Ladder 4 / Engine 10 was on Vinewood Street between West Grand Boulevard and Michigan Avenue, right at the eastern tip of Polonia. When we rolled west, we were in Polonia with not many fires; when we rolled east or north, we were in fire central with all kinds of fires.

The coolest thing about Ladder 4 was that it was a tiller truck (a ladder truck that someone steered the back end). That someone would usually be me. This was an older ladder truck with an open (no roof) tiller bucket, so it was open to rain, snow, heat, and cold, all the elements. I loved it. There are few things more fun than tillering the back end of a fire truck, especially with the sirens and lights are on.

But I started noticing something else on my tiller runs. We weren't just getting fires east anymore. We started getting fires west in Polonia, especially between Junction and Livernois. It started with the party stores.

Party stores are what Detroiters call beer-and-wine or convenience stores. The stores were predominantly owned by people from the Middle East. In the late sixties, right after the 1967 six-day war, thousands of refugees moved to Detroit from the Middle East. Many of them had the same idea. Get a factory job, work hard, save all your money, buy a rundown party store in the city that nobody else wanted, insure it for more than it is worth, burn it down, then get a nice store in the suburbs. It was their American dream, and it worked very well.

The crazy thing was nobody cared! The cops, the insurance companies, nobody seemed to care except us, the firemen. For a while, just about every night at 3:00 a.m., we would get a party store on fire.

After the party store fires came, the garage fires up and down the alleys, then the commercial building fires, then the apartment fires, and finally the dwelling fires. That was saddest of all. It was the same pattern all over Detroit, but now, it was happening to the West Side Polish neighborhood.

There was a wonderful older Polish lady named Wanda who lived on Junction Street. We called her Aunt Wanda. Sometimes she would stop by the firehouse and bring us home-baked cookies or breads, especially around the holidays. When we were out and about doing hydrants and stuff, we would occasionally stop by her house to see if she needed anything. She lived in an immaculate two-story white-frame house with flowers planted all around and a yappy little dog.

One night, we were awakened with the radio call, "Box alarm. Junction and Buchanan." When we pulled up, the vacant house next door to Wanda's was on fire, going throughout, on fire from top to bottom! Wanda was out front screaming with a look of horror on her face that I never forgot. The raging fire was starting to light Wanda's house. We could see the flames getting under her eves. The homes in this area are very close together, only two or three feet apart. Wanda's neighbor was pulling her arm trying to prevent her from running back in. The little dog was barking franticly.

We told Wanda, "It's okay, we got it!" and went to work as fast as we could. But it wasn't okay, and we knew that it wouldn't be. The fire was too far gone. We did a good job saving her house, part of it anyway. We moved as much of her stuff as we could under salvage covers.

Wanda's whole life was that house, that neighborhood, and her church, Saint Francis D'Assisi, which was right around the corner. What ever became of Wanda, I don't know. Just a sad story of a nice old lady who lost her home late one night thanks to some arsonist who never got caught. Just another forgotten old Polish lady and another forgotten Detroit story; this time in what was once known as a beautiful Polish neighborhood.

# Polish: The Last Whites in Detroit

COLEMAN YOUNG, DETROIT'S FIRST BLACK mayor once said, "The only reason I'm mayor of Detroit is that the whites didn't want the damn place anymore." Well, that's not completely true because we Polish still wanted Detroit. It was where we built our homes, our businesses, our clubs, and our churches. Polish people don't run, and we sure weren't the ones who started the white flight.

The Free Press ran a front page story back in 1973 calling the neighborhood west of Southfield and south of Plymouth "Detroit's last white neighborhood." What a coincidence because that's a neighborhood where a lot of Polish lived.

When the great exodus started, I remember many of my white friends and neighbors bailing out. They had many different reasons for moving. Suddenly their house was too small or too big. They were too far from work or something like that. They never said that they moved because of the blacks moving in the neighborhood. Some of them even had those I-Have-a-Dream bumper stickers on their cars. They possibly removed them once they crossed 8 Mile.

It wasn't that they were all racist. Detroit was changing, and the change didn't include whites. It started in July 1967 with the riot. Forty-three people were killed, and two thousand buildings were burned down. After the riot, the politicians seemed to do everything they could for the blacks while getting rid of the whites.

First, Michigan's own former Governor George Romney, who became the Secretary of HUD, sent millions of dollars to the Motor

City to move welfare families from inner city projects into homes in predominantly white Detroit neighborhoods. No money down, and who cares if you ever make a payment. Realtors jumped on the money bandwagon and used illegal blockbusting tactics. They sent out fliers warning of the appending apocalypse to whites who didn't sell their homes and to get the heck out!

Crime was out of control, especially black crime. Detroit became the murder capital of the world. It seemed every week, another white cop was getting shot. Many blacks had organized into groups with scary names like the Black Panthers and the Black Nation of Islam, radicals who wanted their own all-black country. Well, they can't have the country, but how about Detroit?

Then in 1973, Coleman A. Young got elected and made his famous "all crooks hit 8 Mile" speech, many whites thought he meant them.

The final reason for whites to get out of Detroit came in 1975 and that was bussing. Judge Robert E. DeMascio, a Republican who also was the judge in the Algiers Motel incident (the famous trial of a group of white Detroit police officers charged with killing a group of blacks during the riot) ordered Detroit to racially integrate its schools by using bussing. The original suite was for a cross-district bussing plan including Detroit and fifty-three suburban school districts. The Supreme Court rejected it. That left a Detroit-only bussing which did not make sense. Detroit schools at the time had 260,000 students of which 74 percent were black and 26 percent white. Everyone in the city was against it including Coleman Young who called Judge DeMascio a carpetbagger. He knew this would drive the remaining whites out, which it did. In fact today, Detroit Public Schools have less than fifty-two thousand students.

Detroit, once America's fifth largest city, with almost two million people, dropped to 1.5 million in 1970 with only 55 percent white. By 1980, it was down to 1.2 million people of which 34 percent were white. In that 34 percent, there were still a lot of Polish.

Cops and firemen and other city employees who had to live in the city headed toward Detroit's western Polish neighborhood, which was all along Warren Avenue. It became known as copper canyon.

We bought two homes not far from West Warren and not far from my parents' house, who also still lived in the city. Like everyone else in our neighborhood, we sent our kids to a Catholic school: Saint Anselm's in Dearborn Heights. But eventually, we moved out like most of the other whites and some blacks. By 2010, Detroit's population dropped to seven hundred thousand with just 11 percent white.

Today, as I write this, Detroit is going through another change. Millennials, those young folks under thirty-five, are moving back in. Detroit's white population is up to 15 percent; not a lot but better than 11 percent. Old deteriorating neighborhoods are being reclaimed and fixed up. Detroit, which went from a white city to a black city, is now becoming a diverse city, a city for everyone, a city of the future, which can't be a bad thing.

# POLETOWN

DETROIT'S EAST SIDE POLISH NEIGHBORHOOD (Polonia) was the oldest Polish neighborhood in the city. The area was bound by Gratiot on the south, I-75 on the west, Mt. Elliot on the east, and the Hamtramck border on the north. Polish people first moved there in the late 1860s and then established St. Alburtis church in 1870.

This neighborhood become world famous 110 years later in 1980 when the city used eminent domain to tear the neighborhood down so General Motors could use the land for its new assembly plant. General Motors had just closed its last two Detroit factories: the Cadillac Clark street plant and the Fort Street Fleetwood plant.

After World War II, factories in America changed. No longer did American auto companies want the old two-story brick factories that were located throughout the city. They now wanted to build large one-story plants that required one square mile of land. Where does an auto company find a vacant square mile of land in a city?

Factory after factory were moving out of Detroit. Vacant and abandoned old factories were everywhere. Chrysler's Dodge Main plant in Hamtramck, which bordered Poletown, also closed in 1980. When General Motors announced they were closing their last two Detroit factories, the city got desperate. They put together a land package combining the land from the closed Dodge Main plant and the Poletown neighborhood, then offered it to GM for free! "Please build your new factory here."

At the time, Poletown consisted of 4,220 residents, 1,300 homes, 140 businesses, six churches, and one hospital; quite a lot to trade for one factory.

Critics including councilman and former activist Kenny Cockerel said Detroit could locate the new factory in some other less-populated area. Poletown was the last east side ethnic neighborhood in a predominantly black Detroit. But Detroit Mayor Coleman Young disagreed and pulled out all stops using eminent domain to condemn the entire neighborhood and tear it down for General Motors.

The irony in this is that Poletown was located practically next door to the old Black Bottom Hastings Street neighborhood. A thriving all-black neighborhood that was torn down by a white Detroit Mayor in the 1950s to make way for the I-75 freeway. Many people, including Coleman Young, accused Mayor Cobo and the predominantly white city of trying to drive blacks out. Times change and now it was Coleman Young doing the driving and Polish people were the one's getting driven.

Not everyone in Poletown was unhappy. Some residents were happy to sell their home to the city and hit 8 Mile. The neighborhood was deteriorating and most of the young people had moved leaving their parents and grandparents behind. The Catholic Church was happy to unload three old churches that were getting expensive to maintain. The UAW was happy that GM was building a new plant that supposedly would have six thousand jobs. Even Michigan's two senators, Donald Riegle and Carl Levin, refused to intervene.

But many fought to save Poletown. Father Joseph Karasiewicz defied the archbishop and organized a sit in at the Immaculate Conception Church that lasted twenty-nine days. It ended July 14, 1981, when the police forced their way in and arrested Father Karasiewicz and twenty other people.

Father Karasiewicz believed that Archbishop Dearden wanted the church closed right away before his replacement, Bishop Edmond Szoka arrived. Because Bishop Szoka was Polish, he might be more sympathetic to the people of Poletown, and who knows what would have happened?

Ralph Nader (the 1960s activist who ironically was the person that got rid of the Chevy Corvair—a GM product) and his volunteers also showed up and joined in the fight to save Poletown. The whole world started watching.

They took their case to the Michigan Supreme Court and not surprisingly lost. This changed the way the eminent domain laws could be used in the future, which previously could only be used for public projects. Two judges, Fitzgerald and Ryan dissented. They wrote: Eminent domain is a tribute of sovereignty. When citizens are forced to dislocate to permit private companies to build plants, one has to wonder who the sovereign is. No homeowner or business is safe when someone more important comes along.

In 2004, the Michigan Supreme Court, all seven justices voted to overrule the Poletown decision. They stated that cities couldn't use eminent domain to condemn land to be used for private use; a little late for the 4,200 people of Poletown.

Today the General Motors's Detroit Hamtramck Assembly Plant as it's called employs only 1,800 people—4,200 short of the six thousand that had promised. Ironically, 4,200 is the same number of Poletown residents they displaced. Also, Detroit lost one of its last ethnic neighborhoods. A unique thing about Detroit is that it doesn't have any (with the exception of Mexican Town) ethnic neighborhoods. They're all gone. The city never protected them like most other cities do. But Detroit does protect its factories, the one or two that are still there.

# ST. STANISLAUS KOSTKA CHURCH

WHEN WE TALK ABOUT THE Polish Americans and their unique story, we must tell the story of St. Stanislaus, a church located in an old (former) Polish neighborhood in St. Louis, Missouri.

St. Stanislaus is a beautiful red-brick, twin-steeple church built in the Polish cathedral style. It resembles St. Josaphat on Canfield in Detroit. It was built in 1891, north of downtown St. Louis in what was once a thriving Polish neighborhood. St. Stanislaus is considered the best example of a Polish-styled church west of the Mississippi.

Polish Catholics first arrived in St. Louis in the 1860s. They built their little Polonia, and in it, they built four churches: St. Casimir in 1889, St. Hedwig in 1904, Our Lady of Czestochowa in 1906, and the mother church St. Stanislaus.

After the war, the St. Louis Polish, just like Americans everywhere, began leaving the old neighborhood and moving to the suburbs. Attendance at the old churches began dwindling so the archdiocese started closing them down. First St. Casimir's in 1955, then Our Lady of Czestochowa in 1957 and later St. Hedwig in 2005. But when they wanted to close St. Stanislaus, the mother church, something happened. The Polish people from all over St. Louis protested.

They formed a group to save St. Stanislaus, the best of the true Polish parishes. The church that Poland's own Pope John Paul II had visited and said mass at in 1969. The Polish community of metro St. Louis had around sixty thousand people and just about everyone wanted to save St. Stanislaus. They went to the archdiocese with a plan. Polish Catholics from Metro St. Louis would come back and repair, maintain, and pay for the upkeep of the church if the Archdiocese would agree to keep the church open. The bishop agreed.

People from all over St. Louis joined in. They fixed up the church and even bought the land surrounding it. They threw fairs and bake sales and made donations until the church was solvent and self-supporting. It was a source of pride for the St. Louis Poles. They were so successful that the Church's net worth went from practically zero to $8 million.

Eight million! The Archdiocese of St. Louis, it seemed, began to think differently. They informed the people of St. Stanislaus that it was their church and their money, and they wanted both.

It would be hard to see this happening to any other Catholic group of people except the Polish. First, the St. Louis Archdiocese wants to shut down the old Polish Church. Second, the Polish people come together and saved the church, and third, now that the church is saved and worth $8 million, they want it back. Plus who says once the AD took the money that they still wouldn't shut St. Stanislaus down? After all, that was their original intent.

The St. Louis Polish community said no way. It was their church, and whatever money they had raised belonged to the church and not the archdiocese. The excess funds that the parishioners had raised would be put away for future church expenses. To support their argument, the board found a rare agreement from the nineteenth century that gave ownership of the property to the congregation not the archdiocese.

The St. Louis Archdiocese, headed by Archbishop Raymond Leo Burke, tried everything they could to get the church and its assets. They tried to close the church, and when that didn't work, they pulled the priest out. There were no more masses at St. Stanislaus. It was just a place of prayer now. To be fair, the AD needed the money because they had many expenses. The St. Louis Archdiocese, like ADs everywhere, was facing sexual abuse lawsuits (none involving St. Stanislaus priests).

Archbishop Raymond Burke was a man for his times, some might say. He was a man who held many titles with the church. As a trained lawyer, he defended the church both here and in Rome.

Bishop Burke is pretty political for a man of the church. Bishop Burke stated that he would not give communion to Secretary of State John Kerry or any other politician who supported abortion rights.

Bishop Burke became upset when Sheryl Crow, a stem cell advocate, performed at a benefit concert for Cardinal Glennon Children's Hospital. He resigned from the hospital board.

Bishop Burke may be a lot of things, but one thing is he isn't Polish, nor did he seem very sympathetic to the Polish community or their prized church.

After two years without a priest, the St. Stanislaus congregation went out on their own and found a priest, and what a find it was. They found a young priest from Poland named Father Marek Bozek. He was another man for his times, many would say, and perhaps the perfect priest to take on Bishop Burke.

Bishop Burke and the St. Louis Archdiocese went to the (secular) courts to get control of St. Stanislaus. Bishop Burke warned the church not to have mass with their unapproved priest, but they didn't listen. On Christmas Eve 2005, Father Bozek held his first mass at St. Stanislaus, and two thousand people attended.

Bishop Burke went to war. He excommunicated Father Bozek and the entire church board of directors! He then went on and had Father Bozek defrocked as a priest. But that wasn't enough. They tried to have Bozek deported from the United States. All the while, Burke continued his fight in the courts to win back control of St. Stanislaus.

The next thing they attempted was to kick the whole church out of the archdiocese. After 125 years, St. Stanislaus was no longer a Catholic Church. It would no longer be recognized by the Vatican or by the Archdiocese of St. Louis.

St. Stanislaus Church fought on. Father Bozek continued to say mass and give the sacraments even though the defrocked priest was no longer a Catholic. The parishioners split, and some left and joined other Catholic churches. But many stayed and practiced their new Catholic faith with Father Bozek.

March 15, 2012, St. Louis judge, Bryan Hettenbach, ruled in favor of the St. Stanislaus Church Congregation giving them the church and all assets. The judge said, "The archbishop may own the wayward parishioners' souls, but the St. Stanislaus parishioners own the church."

Today the St. Stanislaus Church has around five hundred families. Father Bozek is the pastor. He changed a few things. Gays and divorcees are welcome, and women can serve in the clergy. St. Louis Polish community took a huge risk in this fight with the archdiocese to save this historic church. And Father Bozek, a priest from Poland, also risked everything to save St. Stanislaus church. This only happens in Polonia.

# Paczki Day

THE TUESDAY BEFORE ASH WEDNESDAY has many names: Fat Tuesday, Shrove Tuesday, and Mardi Gras Day, but in Detroit, it's known as Paczki Day.

Paczki or poonchkeys, as we pronounce them, are big jelly doughnuts that Polish love to eat the day before lent. The day after Paczki Day is Ash Wednesday, the day Catholics go to church and get ashes on their foreheads. For the next forty days, Catholics fast for lent. The end of forty days is Easter Sunday.

Paczkis originated in Poland. Just before lent people would get rid of all of their fat and sugar and jam. They would put all that stuff together and make paczkis. The Polish brought that tradition with them when they came to America.

Back in the fifties when I was a kid, only us Polish knew what paczkis were. Back then, there was no Paczki Day or paczki parades or media hype. My mom would go to the Polish bakery on Warren Avenue and buy a dozen prune paczki. If I was lucky, there would be one left over, and the next day, she would pack it in my school lunch. I went to a Catholic school where none of the kids, except for a few Polish, knew what a paczki was.

It's not like that today. Every bakery in Metro Detroit has a paczki sign in their windows on Paczki day. Walmart, Kroger, you name it, now they all make paczkis. The local TV news stations start their morning broadcast from a Polish bakery, interviewing folks lined up to buy a dozen or two paczki. Today all the TV newscasters are paczki eaters from way back, just like us Polish folks.

Paczki aren't just in Detroit. It seems more and more cities all over America are eating paczkis. Buffalo, Chicago, Cleveland, Grand Rapids, and cities in Indiana are eating paczkis on Paczki Tuesday or Shrove Tuesday as some call it. The word shrove, by the way, means repent, which is what we are also supposed to be doing on Paczki Day.

No matter how many cities are eating paczkis, Detroit is number one; ground zero for paczkis. People line up at dawn for paczki at Polish bakeries all over town, including the New Palace or New Martha Washington bakeries in Hamtramck where they have a paczki parade and a paczki queen and king. The city is jumping all day with beer tents, crowded Polish restaurants, and packed bars. Hamtramck is the place to be on Paczki Tuesday, and thousands of people in Metro Detroit make it down there. It's a lot like St. Patrick's Day except everyone is Polish for a day.

When we went to Poland a couple of years ago, we were surprised to find out that the Polish don't eat paczki on Tuesday. They eat them on the Thursday just before lent. Also the paczki in Poland are smaller than ours here in America. I guess everything is bigger in America, even the paczki.

Since I retired, we've been spending our winters in Florida, so we can't make it to Hamtramck for Paczki Day. But we did find a bakery in Venice, Florida, called Yummies, and they make pretty good paczki. On Paczki Day, the place is packed with paczki boxes stacked to the ceiling. Some folks play polka music from their cars out in the parking lot. The owner told me that he is originally from Hamtramck where his grandfather owned a Polish bakery! Paczkis in Florida; who would have believed it?

# CITIES THAT CELEBRATE POLISH HOLIDAYS

BUFFALO, NEW YORK, HAS A big Polish population, and it also celebrates a special day for the Polish called Dyngus Day, which means wet Monday in Poland. It is celebrated on Easter Monday. Boys throw water on girls and spank the back of their legs with pussy willows. Girls also do the same to the boys. Real good-looking girls get drenched on Dyngus Day.

Other American cities also celebrate Dyngus Day, but Buffalo was the first. It started in 1961 with the Chopin Singing Society, a Polish cultural and educational group that dates back to 1899. In 1961, they decided to throw a Dyngus Day party with music and food, and it turned out to be a big success. From that start, it grew over the years to become one of the Buffalo's biggest events.

In Buffalo, they say, everyone is Polish on Dyngus Day. They have a Dyngus parade and parties all over town with polka bands and great Polish food. People dress in red and white—the Polish colors. A very popular drink in Buffalo on Dyngus day is Krupnik Polish liquor. Many people in Buffalo take both Monday and Tuesday off work because the parties last from early morning to the middle of the night.

Cleveland is another city that celebrates Dyngus Day. They have a parade and a Dyngus Day queen. The Cleveland radio stations get involved with fun mischief. In Cleveland, they even have a Polka Hall of Fame to compliment the Rock & Roll Hall of Fame.

South Bend, Indiana, also celebrates Dyngus Day. Festivities in South Bend start at the West Side Democrat Club where the politicians consider Dyngus Day the start of the political season. Many local politicians got their start here on Dingus Day, and many famous politicians came to South Bend to celebrate Dyngus Day. Bill Clinton, Barack Obama, and Bobby Kennedy, to name a few.

Another Polish holiday is Pulaski Day. It is celebrated in many American cities. New York and Philadelphia both have Pulaski Day Parades. They honor Casimir (Kazimierz) Polaski the famous Polish general that France sent here to help us defeat the British and win the Revolutionary War.

In Chicago, the Polish made it an official holiday! It is called Casimir Pulaski Day and is observed the first Monday in March. Chicagoans' idea of a Pulaski Day holiday started back in the 1930s. The Polish who make up a large part of Illinois began to lobby the city and state government for an official holiday, which would become the first and only official Polish holiday in the United States. It took forty years but on September 13, 1977, the Illinois Legislature passed a law making Pulaski Day an official holiday.

The city of Chicago is home to the Polish Museum of America. On Pulaski Day, they have a big party attended by five hundred people. Usually the mayor and many of the Chicago movers and shakers attend.

But it's starting to go down. In 2012, Chicago public schools stopped giving the students a day off on Pulaski Day. One of the reasons given was that the number of Polish kids in Chicago Schools is declining. It seems many Polish Chicagoans are moving to the suburbs just like the Polish in many other cities.

Nothing lasts forever but to have a legal holiday celebrating a Polish general in Illinois is pretty good.

# Mom and Her Sisters Cooking

FEW THINGS MEANT MORE TO Polish women back in the fifties and sixties than cooking. My mom and her three sisters were no exception. All three were great cooks, and all three had their own special recipes. The recipes turned into dishes that would be named after them. The named dishes would be at every family gathering.

Italian women are often credited with being the best cooks, and they certainly are great cooks. Whoever had an Italian friend whose mom wasn't a great cook? But this is a book about the Polish and the Polish women of my mom's generation, who, in my opinion were the best cooks in America.

My mom always made the cheesecake, but it wasn't called cheesecake, or Polish cheesecake, which it certainly was. It was called Henrietta's cheesecake. Her oldest sister, Lillian, always brought Lillian's apple pie—an apple pie baked on a cookie sheet pan that tasted better than any apple pie I ever ate. My mom's second sister, Cassie, always made Aunt Cassie's kapusta, the greatest of all kapusta! Last but not least, my mom's youngest sister, Aunt Irene who always brought Aunt Irene's rolls—homemade bread rolls that would melt in your mouth. Yum!

But it didn't stop at the cooking. Everybody had a garden, a little farm out in the back forty feet (not acres). Relatives stopping by for a visit always started with a walk around the house to view the lawn and flowers then a visit to the garden, which included picking a garden sampler then critiquing it. "These tomatoes are a little bigger than last year's."

Canning was a favorite hobby for Mom and her sisters. It would start with a ride out to the country or to a farmer's market and buy whatever fruit or vegetable that was in season. Pickles, beets, onions, beans, tomatoes, cabbage; you name, they canned it. Aunt Irene and Aunt Cassie both lived close by, and along with mom, the trio would cook and can all day.

Cooking and canning jam was one of my favorites. Peaches in spring and grapes in fall. They would bring home a ton of fruit, and the three of them would peel and chop and cook the fruit in huge pots and then fill up dozens of Mason jars with hot jam. We had a fruit cellar in the basement. The shelves would be stocked full of canned stuff. My mom would send me down there for a jar of peaches or a jar of jam. I think I was fourteen years old before I found out that you could actually buy jam in stores. Okay but not as good-tasting.

Everything my mom and her sisters made was from scratch. No store bought mixes or premade carryout's ever crossed the threshold of any of our homes. Stuff like Kraft Mac & Cheese, TV dinners, SpaghettiOs, and instant mashed potatoes were for other homes not ours. The biggest put-down my mom would make about another women was, "She makes box cakes." No Sara Lee box cake ever graced our pantry shelves.

When the holidays came, things got crazy. Mom and her sisters would get together and cook for days! They loved cooking, and as a young kid, I loved watching them. Fruitcakes baked in buttered brown paper-lined loaf pans, pierogi made with farmer's cheese and hundreds of Christmas cookies. Kolacky filled with homemade jam, sugar cookies in every different Christmas shape, and my favorite, springerle or anise cookies as we sometimes called them. Lucky for me, my wife Linda, still makes them using the springerle rolling pin that my mom gave her years ago.

I would stand out of the way watching them work and laughing at their funny stories just waiting for them to toss me a reject.

Polish men never did any of the cooking back then, they just ate, although my father, to his credit, did cook two dishes: French toast made with flour in the batter and potato pancakes. My father and uncles did do two things food related: worked in their gardens and picked mushrooms.

My dad's garden was perfect: no weeds and a little handmade fence he put up to try to keep the rabbits out. Spring was mushroom-hunting season. My dad and his brother Wesley would go off to Rouge Park and bring back boxes full of mushrooms. We would fry them up in butter; Polish strawberries we called them. Later in life, I found out that you had to be careful because some might be poisonous. They must have known what they were doing because none of us died.

Over the years, many other family members find themselves with food dishes named after them. My cousin Josephine was also known for the Polish cheesecake. Another relative, Vicky, is known for Vicky's beans. Nancy, my sister, is recognized for her excellent kapusta. Lately, her daughter, Tracy, is also doing the kapusta. Nowadays my wife, Linda, is the Polish cheesecake queen (made with farmer's cheese). And I'm always asked to make the sheet apple pie, but we still call it Lillian's apple pie, not Bob's.

After us older kids had grown and moved away, my mom looked for something to do. Mom loved to cook, and people would often comment on how good Henrietta's (or Dixie as she was sometimes called) cooking was. One day, Mom was asked to cook for a First Communion party. She called her good friend, Helen, and the two of them cooked up an excellent Polish dinner for fifty people. That's how it started. Before you knew it, Helen and Mom had a little Polish catering company that was catering weddings and parties at all the little halls in the neighborhood. Every catering job led to one or two more. After a few years, the work and the arthritis caught up with her, and she hung up her catering apron. Mom wasn't just a good Polish cook but also a professional Polish cook known throughout the neighborhood!

# GREAT POLISH
# PEOPLE

# Paul Landowski

ONE OF THE THINGS ON my bucket list is to travel to the city of Rio de Janeiro, not for the beaches but to see the magnificent statue named Christ the Redeemer—the statue of Jesus Christ perched high on a mountain overlooking the city and harbor of Rio.

It is an amazing work of art built on a 2,300-foot peak of the Corcovado Mountain. It reaches 125 feet in height and weighs 635 metric tons. The statue has Christ holding out his hands in the shape of the cross. It is one of the most recognized symbols of Christianity in the world and one of the seven wonders of the modern world. The person who built this statue is a Polish sculptor named Paul Landowski.

Paul Landowski was a famous sculptor who lived in France. He was born in 1875 and died in 1961. Paul graduated from the French National Academy and has sculpted thirty-five monuments in Paris alone. His career lasted for thirty-five years.

The idea for the Christ the Redeemer statue started in Rio in 1920. Catholics in Brazil went out in the streets for a week and collected money. The week was called monument week. In that one week, they collected an amazing $250,000 dollars, which is equivalent to $3,500,000 in today's money. Paul Landowski started the statue in 1922, and it took nine years to create. The statue opened on October 12, 1931.

# CASIMIR FUNK

TAKE YOUR VITAMINS LIKE MOM always said. Well, if you do take vitamins, you can thank a Polish researcher named Casimir (Kazimierz) Funk who invented vitamins in 1912.

The way Casimir invented vitamins was in his research, He found that people who ate brown rice instead of white rice were less vulnerable to beriberi, a nutritional disorder caused by the lack of thiamine. Funk tried to find and isolate what substance was in brown rice that white rice didn't have. He succeeded and called it amine or B3. He then added the word vit for vitality and coined the word vitamin.

Funk didn't stop at beriberi. He knew that there must be other diseases that his vitamins could cure. He found cures for many other ailments such as rickets, a disease caused by the lack of vitamin D. The disease scurvy, was a big problem to sailors sailing the seas. Funk figured out that it was caused by the lack of vitamin C. In 1940, Funk moved to America and spent the rest of his life researching the causes of cancer.

# Madame Curie

MADAME CURIE WAS THE FIRST woman to win a Nobel Prize, and the only woman to win it twice!

She was born Marie Sklodowski in Warsaw, Poland, on November 7, 1867. She studied at the Polish Flying University, a secret university in Warsaw. The Russians who controlled Poland at that time made it difficult for Polish people to get a higher education, so the Poles formed secret colleges called Flying Universities where Curie and many other Polish had to do their studies.

In 1891, to be free of Russian control, she moved to Paris where she met and married another physicist named Pierre Curie. In Paris, Curie discovered and coined the word radioactivity. She invented ways to isolate radioactive isotopes and discovered two elements: polonium (which she named after Poland) and radium. She also founded the Curie Institute in Paris and Warsaw.

Madame Curie is the inventor of the x-ray machine. During World War I, Madame took her new invention to the battle front were she selflessly performed thousands of x-rays on wounded soldiers saving many lives but exposing herself to great deals of radiation. She died in 1934 at the age of sixty-six from exposure to radiation.

# HENRYK SIENKIEWICZ

HENRYK SIENKIEWICZ WAS A POLISH writer and journalist best known for writing *Quo Vadis* in 1896. He was awarded the Nobel Prize for literature in 1908. In his native land of Poland, he is best known for a trilogy of novels: *With Fire and Sword, The Deluge*, and *Sir Michael*. All have been made into films.

Henryk live in partitioned Poland and often criticized the Russians and the Germans for their persecution of the Polish especially for banning the Polish language and not allowing it to be taught in schools. When World War I broke out, he moved to Switzerland where he died in 1916.

His famous novel, *Quo Vadis*, which also became a film, was about early Christians in Rome and their struggle against Emperor Nero. It was thought to parallel the Polish people and their struggles against their oppressors in occupied Poland. It was also a critique against materialism and decadence in early Christianity.

# Nicholas Copernicus

Nicholas Copernicus was a Polish astronomer; the greatest astronomer ever. He is the one who first discovered that the Earth goes around the sun. Not only was Copernicus the greatest astronomer, but also, he was one of history's greatest economists who discovered Gresham's Law or Quantity Theory of Money that bad money drives out good money. He was also a doctor and a couple of other things, but astronomy is what this genius is best known for!

Copernicus lived in the sixteenth century in a town called Warmia in what was called Polish Prussia. It was a place that was always being attacked and ransacked by the Teutonic Knights. Copernicus was a Catholic, which made it a little rough when Prussia turned Protestant. He traveled to Rome where he met Pope Clement VII and several cardinals and explained his theory of the Earth going around the sun, not the other way around, which is what they believed at the time. Surprisingly, they were receptive at first.

Here are the seven principles of Copernicus's theory:

1. Planets don't revolve around one fixed point.
2. Earth is not the center of the universe.
3. The sun is the center, and all celestial bodies rotate around it.
4. The distance between sun and Earth is only a tiny fraction of the distance between the sun and other stars.
5. The stars don't move. They only look like their moving because the Earth is constantly rotating.
6. Earth moves in a circle around the sun causing the sun's perceived yearly movement.

7.   Earth's own movement causes other planets to appear to move in an opposite direction.

All seven of these facts, which seem so common sense to us now, were unheard of and shocking to the world back then. This was all written in a book called *De Revolutionibus Orbium Coelestium*, which means revolutions of heavenly spheres. The book was presented for the first time to Copernicus on his deathbed where he reportedly woke up, saw it, and died.

Most people didn't believe Copernicus and his theory. As always, the ignorant made fun of him. They even made a comedy called *The Foolish Sage* about the silly astronomer who stops the sun and moves the Earth.

The churches also attacked Copernicus and called it heresy, but surprisingly not just the Catholics, but the Protestants were also narrow-minded and maybe even more so.

Martin Luther called the book heresy. Luther's assistant, a Lutheran minister named Andreas Osiander went further. He forged an entry into the book supposedly by Copernicus himself that said none of this it true. Copernicus on his deathbed couldn't fight it. The book was published in 1543, and the Catholic Church banned it in 1616.

# THE BAD POLISH

# LEON CZOLGOSZ

KILLING SOMEONE IS ALWAYS BAD, but killing the President of the United States is really bad. Four American presidents have been assassinated and one of them by a Polish American. His name was Leon Czolgosz.

Leon Czolgosz was born in Alpena, Michigan, in 1873. He was the son of Paul Czolgosz and Mary "Nowak" Czolgosz. Leon grew up in Detroit and Posen, Michigan, where his parents owned a farm. Leon was fairly smart, attending the University of Michigan for a while. Leon ended up getting a job in a steel mill along with his brothers. In 1898, an economic crash hit the country and millions of people lost jobs, including Leon and his brothers. Leon and his brothers looked for work, but there was nothing out there.

Leon then became a radical, attending meetings and reading radical literature. He blamed the problems of the country on the disparity of wealth between the rich and the poor. He also blamed the rich elitists, including President William McKinley.

William McKinley was born in Ohio in 1843. He joined the Union Army as a private in the Civil War where he rose to the rank of major. After the war, he became a lawyer and then a politician and then Governor of Ohio. In 1897, William McKinley was elected the twenty-fifth president of the United States. He was reelected in 1901.

McKinley had huge accomplishments. He was president during the Spanish-American War. For winning the war, the US got Puerto Rico, the Philippines, and Guam. The US also kicked the Spaniards out of Cuba—Cuba Libre. He then annexed Hawaii where he said, "If we don't, Japan will. We need Hawaii more then we need

California!" McKinley put the US on the gold standard. He also put tariffs on imported goods to help save American industry.

On September 6, 1901, President William McKinley and Leon Czolgosz both went to Buffalo, New York, to attend the Pan American Exposition. President McKinley was shaking hands. Leon got in line, and when he reached the front, McKinley stuck out his hand to shake. Czolgosz brushed it aside and pulled out a .32-caliber pistol he had bought for $4.50. He then shot McKinley two times in the stomach. The police tackled Czolgosz. McKinley looked up and said, "Go easy on him, boys!"

McKinley died two weeks later on September 14, 1901. Theodore Roosevelt, his vice president, succeeded him. Cosgrosz was tried and found guilty on September 24, 1901. He was sentenced to death on October 29, 1901, less than two months after he shot McKinley. Czolgrosz was electrocuted. His last request, to see his father, was denied.

# HYMIE WEISS

HYMIE WEISS WAS ONE OF the most notorious Chicago gangsters of the Roaring Twenties. He was supposedly the only man Al Capone feared.

Hymie's original name was Earl Wojciechowski. He was born on January 25, 1898, as a Polish American and a Catholic (despite his Jewish-sounding nickname). Hymie regularly went to church and always carried his rosary along with his 1911 Colt .45 Automatic Pistol.

Hymie grew up on the North Side of Chicago where he started out a petty thief as a teenager and grew to become the head of the North Side mob, which numbered in the hundreds. They controlled all the bootlegging on the North Side of Chicago while Al Capone and his gang controlled the bootlegging on the South Side.

Hymie Weiss became the leader of the North Siders because he was a psychopath murderer who even shot his own brother. Hymie had no problem pulling the trigger and was feared by all, including Capone. Hymie was a big reason Capone didn't take over the North Side of Chicago.

The North Siders were mostly Polish and Irish while Capone's South Siders were mostly Italian. The two gangs had a big disagreement over prostitution. Hymie Weiss and his Polish and Irish gangsters were against prostitution while Capone and his Italian gangsters not only supported it but also controlled the whorehouses in Chicago, some of which were on the North Side.

The two gangs violently fought each other over the years. Hymie made repeated attempts on Capone's life, killing many of his South

Side gangsters in the process, but he never got Capone. In the end, Capone won. On October 11, 1926, Capone's gangsters ambushed Hymie and four other gang members outside a flower shop on State Street. In one of the most famous shootings in Chicago history, using Thompson machine guns, they mowed them down killing Weiss.

Hymie's life may have ended that day, but his spirit lives on. The actor James Cagney based his famous gangster characters on Hymie Weiss. Hymie suffered from severe migraine headaches, and Cagney even used that in a movie. That famous movie line "Take him for a ride" came from Hymie.

# John Wayne Gacy

JOHN WAYNE GACY (GATZA), THE original killer clown, was a Polish Catholic (half Polish) who was born in Chicago on March 17, 1942. His father was Polish and was said to be very mean to him. Maybe that's one of the reasons John would become one of the most vicious killers in the United States.

John grew up, got married, and moved to Iowa where he became a successful businessman. Then in 1968, John was sent to prison for ten years for molesting a teenage boy. His wife divorced him. John ended up only serving eighteen months of a ten-year rap. They said he was a model prisoner. John always found a way to beat the system.

After his release from prison, John moved back to the Chicago area and, along with his mother, bought a home at 8213 Summerdale Avenue in Norwood Park Township. This home would later become the infamous house of horrors. John got married a second time and had two children. Shortly after John's second marriage, his mother moved out.

John started a successful business called PDM Contractors. He would remodel, fix, and maintain homes and businesses. John employed a lot of young men including teens.

Besides running his business, John got very involved in the community. He joined the Jaycees and became one of its leaders. He served on a Norwood Park Township Commission. He joined the local moose and became a clown on its Jolly Joker clown team. They would perform at children's hospitals and various charity events all over Chicago. From 1975 to 1978, John was the director of the annual Polish Constitution Day Parade. Beyond any doubt, John was a pillar of the community!

On January 2, 1972, while his wife and kids were out of town, John picked up a sixteen-year-old boy from Michigan named Timothy McCoy. John took him back to his house where he raped him and murdered him. John said he didn't mean to kill him, but it gave him the greatest thrill of his life. This was Gacy's first murder, and he loved it. He knew he found his calling in life. Shortly afterward, he told his wife that he was a homosexual and wanted a divorce. His wife divorced him and, along with the kids, moved out. The house was all his.

The house at 8213 Summerdale Avenue became a house of horrors. He would usually bring young boys back there and get them drunk or high and then he would start joking around like the clown he was. He would talk them into letting him handcuff them and then it was all over. He would first rape them and then he would torture them, often until they begged to die. Then he would tie a rope around their poor neck and strangle them. After he killed them, he would drag their nude, mutilated body to bed and spend the rest of the night sleeping with the corpse. The next day, he would bury them in the crawl space under his house. Altogether, he killed thirty-three young men, every single one at 8213 Summerdale.

The boys came from all over. Some were homeless, but many came from good families. Some of his victims were his employees at PDM. How could he get away with this? Where were the authorities while this was going on? That is the second part of this horror story.

Many times, the local police were notified, but nothing happened. Gacy was a pillar of the community and a great bullshitter. John would just give them some story that the kid must be a run away or something, and the cops bought it every time. One time, a victim somehow managed to escape and went to the cops but to no avail.

Gacy's third victim was a seventeen-year-old named John Butkovitch. He worked for Gacy at PDM and went to Gacy's home to pick up a check and was never heard from again. Butkovitch's parents called the police, and they went over and talked to Gacy who said the young man picked up his check and said he was going to run away. Again, the police believed Gacy and let it go. The parents didn't believe this bullshit for a minute. For the next three years, they called the police one hundred times saying Gacy is a murderer who killed their son. The pain that family must have felt, and what frustration they must have toward that police department. And how many lives were lost by their inaction?

But as with all things in life, Gacy's luck was about to run out. Gacy ran out of space under his house, so he decided to start dumping the bodies in the Des Plaines River. Now the Des Plaines Police Department was involved, and if there is any hero in this story, it is the detectives who work there.

On December 11, 1978, Gacy went to a drugstore in Des Plaines to bid a job. He noticed a young man working there: a fifteen-year-old boy named Robert Priest. Gacy approached him and offered him a job at PDM paying twice as much as the drugstore job. They arranged to meet later and talk it over. Robert Priest would be Gacy's last victim.

When Robert didn't come home, his parents called the Des Plaines Police Department. They drove out to Norwood Park to talk to Gacy. He gave them his usual BS, "The kid must have run away," but it didn't work with these guys. They looked up his record and were astonished to find out he was a convicted sexual molester, a state-certified psychopath, and had numerous other complaints against him. These cops stayed on Gacy 24-7 following his every move and harassing him whenever they could. Gacy went so far as to have his lawyers file a harassment complaint against the DPPD.

The cops beat Gacy's lawyers to the punch by getting a judge to sign a search warrant for 8213 Summerdale Avenue where they discovered the unthinkable twenty-nine bodies buried under the house plus four more that Gacy threw in the river.

Gacy went to trial where he tried every trick in the book to save himself. In the end, Gacy was sentenced to death. Gacy told the judge, "Killing me will not bring back those boys!" On May 10, 1994, John Wayne Gacy was executed by the State of Illinois. His last words were "Kiss my ass!"

# Unabomber

BORN THE SAME YEAR AND from the same town as John Wayne Gacy is another one of our bad Polish persons. Ted Kaczynski was born in Chicago on May 22, 1942, to Theodore and Wanda Kaczynski.

Kaczynski was a bright little kid from day one with a 167 IQ. Growing up in Chicago, he skipped two grades of school. In 1958 at the age of sixteen, he went to Harvard. Four years later, he went to the University of Michigan and earned his doctorate degree. After Michigan in 1967, Ted headed out west to California were he got a position teaching at the University of California Berkley.

Ted Kaczynski only stayed at Berkley for two years. He left and moved to Montana where he built a cabin in the woods. Ted planned to have a simple life in his cabin, living off the land. But the world started to close in around him. Ted became anti-government and anti-technology. Ted started to do crazy things.

In 1978, Ted Kaczynski sent a package bomb to North Western University where a security guard was injured opening the package. In 1979, Ted tried to blow up an American Airlines 727, but luckily, the bomb didn't go off. After that, the FBI named him the Unabomber, which stands for universities and airlines. Between the years 1978 and 1995, Ted is accredited with sixteen bombs, which killed three people and injured twenty-three.

In 1995, Ted Kaczynski sent out a thirty-five-thousand-word manifesto about his disagreements with our society. His brother, David, read it and knew Ted wrote it. He notified the FBI who raided his cabin where they found numerous bombs, records, and journals. Their seventeen-year search for the Unabomber was over. Ted was arrested, and in 1998, was sentenced to life in prison. This was the longest and costliest investigation in FBI history.

# POPE JOHN PAUL II

WHO BETTER TO FOLLOW A chapter on the bad Polish than the best Polish person of my lifetime, Pope John Paul II.

Pope John Paul I died after only being pope for a month. In October 1978, all the cardinals traveled to Rome to pick a new pope. Catholics all over the world stood by watching the TV coverage from the Vatican, waiting for the smoke to change color. When it finally changed color, everyone wondered which Italian cardinal would be the new pope. It was always an Italian. After all, it's called the Church of Rome.

Not this time. To the surprise of every Catholic and a lot of non-Catholics and for the first time in five hundred years, the pope would not be Italian. The new pope would be from another country. It was not just any country. The new pope would be from Poland. Get out the vodka, fry up the pierogis, turn up the polkas; the new pope is Polish!

Karol Wojtyla was born on May 18, 1920, in Wadowice, Poland, to Karol and Emilia (Kaczorowska) Wojtyla. His mother was a schoolteacher and died when Karol was eight. He had a brother, Edward, who became a doctor. Edward, who was thirteen years older than Karol, died of scarlet fever when Karol was thirteen.

Growing up, Karol, was a robust young man who loved sports and the outdoors. He was also a good student. When Karol was eighteen, he moved to Krakow to attend the famous Jagiellonian University where he studied philosophy while learning twelve different languages. All Polish boys at that time had mandatory military training; Karol was assigned to the Academic Legion of the Thirty-

Ninth Infantry Division. While in training. Karol refused to fire a gun and was soon sent back.

Then in September 1939, the Germans invaded Poland changing Karol and Poland's way of life. The Germans shut down the universities and started deporting young men to Germany to work in slave camps. To avoid this, Karol got menial jobs. In 1941, his father died. Karol was alone now and decided to become a priest. The Germans also closed down the seminaries, so Karol was forced to study for the priesthood underground.

Bad things came in threes to Karol. Vehicles hit him three different times: twice in 1940 by a truck and then by a streetcar. Then in 1944, Karol was run over by a German Army truck. Badly injured, the Germans took him to an Army field hospital. Karol would suffer back and neck problems from this accident for the rest of his life. Karol was also involved at this time with helping Jews escape from the Nazis.

Karol was ordained a priest in the Metropolitan Cathedral on Wavell Hill on November 1, 1946. He was then sent to Rome to study philosophy. He also studied in Belgium and France. After returning to Poland, he was assigned to a parish near Krakow. At this time when the newly ordained Father Wojtyla arrived in Poland, Hitler and the Nazis were replaced by Stalin and the communists.

Almost overnight, Father Wojtyla became one of Poland's most famous priests. The people who came from all over to attend his masses loved his powers of oratory and his vocabulary, which was said to be poetic. Father Wojtyla also used his pulpit on occasion to speak out against their communist oppressors.

On July 4, 1958, Father Wojtyla was appointed Auxiliary Bishop of Krakow. He was only thirty-eight years old and became Poland's youngest bishop. Five years later in 1963, he became an archbishop. Four years after that on June 26, 1967, Pope Paul VI gave him his red hat, and he became Cardinal Wojtyla. Then on October 16, 1978, he was elected pope and took the name John Paul II.

Pope John Paul II became a very popular pope who was loved by people everywhere. He traveled to 129 different countries bringing the word of God to millions. He fought for the poor and the oppressed and helped in the defeat of communism by helping Poland to form the Solidarity Party. He was brave, and three attempts were made on his life.

Bad things come in threes especially to Pope John Paul II, but to survive three assassination attempts is a miracle. The first assassination attempt was on May 13, 1981; He was shot by a Turkish gunman. The gunman named Mehmet Ali Agca was said to have been sent by the Russians to stop the pope's meddling in the Solidarity movement. Pope John Paul survived.

The second attempt happened exactly two years later on May 12, 1983, in Fatima, Portugal. This time, a crazed Spanish priest named Juan Fernandez Krohn stabbed the pope with a World War II German bayonet. Pope John Paul again escaped death. The assassin also managed to escape prison; he was kicked out of the priesthood and kicked out of Portugal. He moved to Belgium, became a lawyer, and then supposedly tried to kill the king, Albert II. Again, no jail time.

The third assassination attempt happened in June of 1995 in the Philippines. Pope John Paul was there to help celebrate World Youth Day. Ramzi Yousef, the terrorist mastermind of the World Trade Center bombing, was there with a plan to assassinate the pope. A suicide bomber was to dress as a priest concealing a bomb hidden under his frock. When he got close to the pope, he would detonate the bomb killing Pope John Paul and everyone else around including himself.

Shortly before the pope's arrival, the Fire Department got a call to an apartment building about a strange order. The Fire Department investigated, found nothing, and made it a false alarm. A detective named Aida Fariscal reviewed the false alarm report and realized that the apartment building was the same one that a group of suspicious Arabs lived in. She got a bunch of cops, and they kicked in the apartment door and found a bomb-making operation, a priest outfit, and a laptop, which made this one of the greatest terrorist findings ever.

The laptop belonged to none other than Ramzi Yousef, the Al Quada terrorist mastermind. The laptop not only detailed the planned assassination of Pope John Paul but also plans to hijack eleven commercial airliners in a day of terror and also the plan to hijack jet planes and crash them into the World Trade Center. They saved the pope, but unfortunately, Ramzi Yousef got away. Also, as we know, the World Trade Center attack still happened six years later.

September 18, 1987, Pope John Paul II visited Detroit, and I was there. Every Polish Catholic was there! It was huge! The pope arrived at Metro Airport Friday September 18 at 9 p.m. on his private jet called Shepherd One. He departed Saturday at 8 p.m. for a total Detroit stay of twenty-three hours. It was a very busy twenty-three hours that included a motorcade that started in Hamtramck and ended with a mass at the Silverdome.

The mass at the Silverdome included people from every one of Detroit's 345 parishes. You needed a ticket to get in, and Father Maloney from Saint Anselm hooked me up with two main floor tickets. How lucky. Thanks, Father. I took my dad. My dad is the most Catholic man I have ever known. What a treat it was for him at seventy-three years old to see the Holy Father.

We left way early for the Silverdome and still almost didn't get there. The freeway was a parking lot. The Silverdome holds eighty thousand, but they must have packed in one hundred thousand to see the pope. I never saw it so crowded. We made it just in time.

It was magnificent. One thing I must say about Detroit, my hometown, whenever they do something like this, they do it first class. They had a large altar in the center made of a beautiful lightwood. The choir consisted of 1,200 people, and they almost blew the dome off the Silverdome. I had never seen so many red hats or priests or nuns. It was a great day to be Catholic.

Then the pope entered. He was riding in that funny little popemobile. He circled the entire Silverdome giving everyone his blessing. I had the feeling one must have when they are in the presence of a saint. Mass was held, and we went to communion. Afterward, the pope left in his popemobile. Gone, but he will be with me forever.

On April 2, 2005, Pope John Paul II died. He was the second longest-serving pope in history—twenty-seven years. He was also one of the hardest-working popes. He was a tireless defender of life and humanity, wrote books about Catholic topics, and pleaded always for world peace. He made more saints than any other pope, and it was said that he was the most recognized man on the face of the Earth. He was canonized by Pope Francis on April 27, 2014, in Saint Peter's Square. Five hundred thousand people attended.

# SOLIDARITY

GROWING UP IN THE 50S and 60s, nothing scared us more than Russia. It was the Cold War, and those god-hating, freedom-hating commies with all their nuclear missiles were out to destroy us. We grew up with backyard bomb shelters, air raid drills at school and Nike missiles in our parks.

It was the American way of life. We called it the Cold War. The world was divided in two halves: one half was America, the good guys, and the other half was Russia, the bad guys. There were two red buttons: one in Washington and one in Moscow; pushing either one would fire the nukes and bring the end of the world.

This was the way it was, and we thought the world would be this way forever. Then in 1989, the Berlin Wall fell, and with it, the Soviet Union and communism. That was one of the most amazing happenings in my lifetime, and like a lot of people, I wondered how this could have happened. One big reason that communism fell was Poland where a group of workers formed a trade union that stood up to Russia and its puppet government in Poland.

It can't be said enough, and it should never be forgotten. World War II started with Germany taking over Poland and ended with Russia taking Poland as the rest of the world, including America, stood by and watched. But the Russian takeover never went smoothly. Those troublesome Polish fought them any way that they could.

The communist persecuted the Polish people and the Catholic Church. In 1953, they arrested Cardinal Stefan Wyszynski and confined him to a monastery. In 1956 during a demonstration in Poznan, the police opened fire, killing seventy-five and injuring hundreds more. In 1976, strikes and riots in Poland resulted in economic crises. Then came the big one.

In 1980, protesting high food prices, seventeen-thousand workers at the Lenin Shipyards in Gdańsk, Poland went on strike. Strikes were illegal in communist Poland. They barricaded themselves inside the shipyard. Lech Walesa, a fired former worker, became their leader. They presented the communist government with a list of demands that included religious freedom, political freedom, independent unions, and better pay. They called themselves Solidarnosc or Solidarity.

From the shipyards of Gdańsk to the rest of Poland, Solidarity grew. By 1981, it had ten million members: ten million out of a country of thirty million, one-half of the work force. This was the first opposition movement to Russia of any Soviet Bloc Nation.

The communist government struck back, and in 1981, Poland's puppet leader, Wojciech Jaruzelski, declared martial law! Solidarity was named an illegal organization, and its leaders were rounded up and sent to prison.

But this did not stop Solidarity. They went underground and continued their fight. Then in 1988, Solidarity came above ground and called for a nationwide strike. Poland shut down, and amazingly, the Russians backed down; they did not roll their tanks or try to stop Solidarity. After forty-five years of fighting the Polish, the Russians had enough. This was the start of the end of the Soviet Union and the end of the Cold War. All thanks to a group of brave Polish union workers.

In 1989, Poland had their first free election in forty-five years. The country threw out their former communist party leaders and elected a Solidarity government. They also threw out their constitution written by the communist in 1952 and wrote a new one. Lech Walesa was elected president, their first non-communist leader since World War II.

Lech Walesa is an interesting fellow. He was born in 1943 in Popowo, Poland, during the Nazi occupation. His father was sent to a labor camp and died shortly after the war ended. His mother, who would die years later in a car wreck in New Jersey, raised him. Lech became an electrician, and in 1967, got a job at the Lenin Shipyards in Gdańsk. Lech married Miroslana Danota Golos in 1969, and together, they had eight children.

Lech got involved in union issues right away. He was a natural-born leader and very charismatic. In 1976, Lech's union activity got him fired. He did odd jobs to survive while organizing unions and strikes. Lech did most of his union stuff underground.

Then in 1980 when the Lenin shipyard workers went on strike, Lech climbed the fence and took over. After the strikers won and Solidarity spread all over Poland, Lech their leader became a national hero.

In 1989 after the fall of communism, Lech ran for president with the slogan, "I don't want to, but I have to." Lech won and became Poland's first non-communist head of state in forty-five years. As president, he switched Poland to a free market economy, kicked out the Russian troops (who were there to protect Poland from an American invasion), and joined NATO.

After a few years, Lech's popularity started to slip. He made abortions, that always had been legal and favored by the majority, illegal. He called gays sick and said they had no right to hold office. He staffed his cabinet with old friends that some people thought were unqualified thugs. People thought Lech to be uneducated and undignified. In 1993, Lech called for a union between Poland and Germany. How crazy was that? Then credible allegations came out that Lech, at one time, might have been an informant to the communist. Lech's popularity slipped to 10 percent, and in 1995, he was thrown out of office.

But if the Polish people lost their love of Lech, the rest of the world didn't. *Time Magazine* named him man of the year. He has forty-five honorary doctorates from universities all over the world, including Harvard. In 1989, he received the Presidential Medal of Freedom. Last but not least, the rock group U2's big hit, "New Year's Day," is about Lech Walesa.

# CHRISTMAS

AN IRISH FRIEND ONCE TOLD me that his favorite day of the year was St. Patrick's Day. All right, that makes sense. Polish people, if asked what their favorite day is, would overwhelmingly say Christmas. I don't think there is another nationality that treasures Christmas more than the Polish. We get that distinct Christmas feeling, and it doesn't matter where we are or whom we're with, there's nothing like Christmas. Let us see a star in the sky or hear a carol or even an old Christmas movie on TV, and we're there. Christmas is magic to every Pole. It's our biggest day.

Christmas in Poland is a three-day affair (like so many things in Polish culture). It starts on Christmas Eve, which they call Wigilia, a Polish word derived from Latin meaning to stand night guard. They have a huge twelve-course meatless dinner where the main course is carp. Not ordinary Detroit River-style carp, but a special Christmas carp that they buy, live days before, and keep in a tub of fresh water to soak all the impurities out.

The table is set with their very best and under the tablecloth is straw to remind them of the stable where Jesus was born. They leave an empty chair for a deceased love one's spirit to join them. Christmas Eve dinner is never started until the first star is in the sky.

Distributing the oplatek always starts Polish Christmas dinner. Oplatek is a thin wafer made of flour and water, usually with religious symbols on one side. It symbols peace, forgiveness, and good luck for the coming year. The head of the family starts by breaking off a piece and wishing his family good health and a wonderful Christmas. He then eats that piece and passes the wafer to the next member and then the next. Each person wishes greetings until the last person has had a piece of the wafer and then dinner is served.

Polish farmers even serve oplatek to their farm animals. This goes back to the Middle Ages where it is believed that animals can talk on Christmas Eve. If you don't hear them talk, too bad, because it is also believed that only the pure of heart can hear.

After dinner, everyone goes to midnight mass called pasterka or Shepherd's Mass.

On Christmas Day, children wake up to presents given to them by Jesus, not Santa Claus. The day is spent with friends and family enjoying homemade cookies and pastries made special for Christmas.

The third day of Christmas is the day after Christmas or December 26. This day is a legal holiday in Poland. Everyone has the day off, but it is not called Boxing Day as it is in England and Canada. It is called St. Stephen Day. St. Stephen was the first Christian martyr, and the day is named after him. Polish young people head to the taverns on St. Stephen's Day for a third day of rivalry.

Growing up on Orangelawn, we always had a wonderful Christmas. About a month before Christmas, the first day the Christmas tree lots opened, my dad would run out and get our tree. He had to have the best tree; the pick of the lot. He'd also get extra branches that he used to fill in the bare spots. Dad would drive home with it tied up on the car roof. He would drag the tree to the backyard, then stand it up in the yard next to the garage. It would stay there until two days before Christmas when he would drag it inside the living room and put on the lights. Then us, excited kids, would put on the ornaments and tinsel.

My friends would already have their Christmas tree up for weeks by the time we put ours up. This was the old Polish way. The Christmas tree went up on Christmas Eve and stayed up until Epiphany, January 6, or Three Kings' Day as my mom called it. Two things are found on every Polish Christmas tree: a Polish Christmas ornament (Poland makes the best Christmas ornaments in the world) and a nativity scene underneath.

As a kid, we would head up to the stores on Plymouth Road to do our Christmas shopping. My young funds were somewhat limited, just a few bucks I earned raking leaves or shoveling snow. I stretched my money the best I could doing most of my shopping at Woolworths. The stores would be decorated for the holidays with Christmas music playing over the PA. Klein's department store would even fly in a Santa in a helicopter. I never missed that big event.

Regrettably, my family didn't have a celebration on Christmas Eve like most people; we saved that for Christmas Day. But Christmas Eve was still exciting. We would fast until the first star was in the sky. Also, we were always observant for a knock on our back door by a hungry stranger because it could be Jesus in disguise.

Waking up on Christmas Day would be magic! Underneath the tree would be a gift for each of us; whatever we asked for. It was the only day of the entire year we would ever get a toy. My favorite gift ever was a Lionel train set that I still have today. We would then put on our new Christmas outfit and pile into the car for Christmas mass. I would always run into a friend or two and ask, "What did you get?"

After mass, we would come home to our Christmas dinner, Krakus Polish ham and all the fixings. My mom would bake tons of delicious cookies and the world's best fruitcakes. We still bake fruitcakes every Christmas using Mom's recipe. After dinner, we would again all pile into the car and head over to our aunts', uncles', and cousins' homes, or they would come to ours. Christmas isn't Christmas without your relatives, especially for us Polish. It was always a late night and a great night, and we stretched every minute out of it.

Detroit was the place to be at Christmas. We were a rich area, and we showed it. We had a big round building in Dearborn called the Ford Rotunda. It was the fifth most popular tourist destination in America. Every year, they put on a fantastic Christmas display. They had a thirty-five-foot Christmas tree surrounded by little mechanical elves. It was like Disneyland's It's a Small World, only better. The girls loved the hundreds of dolls on display. I loved the train layout. Ford would display their new cars: cool T-Birds with the tops down; they even had Santa driving one. It was the number one Christmas show in America.

We always would head Downtown to a lit up Christmas fantasy. The streets and buildings were all decorated, and in the center was one of the biggest department stores in the world. J. L. Hudson Department Store with eight stories of Christmas tree lights on its front. The windows were decorated using animated figures. The twelfth floor was called Toyland and was every Detroit kid's mecca.

Ford Rotunda burned down in 1962 as they were preparing the Christmas display. Five years later, a good portion of Detroit burned down. Then in in 1997, they imploded the J. L. Hudson Building, which was closed since 1983. All the old Christmas stuff was gone.

People then turned to the local malls where they settled for a mall Santa and a small Christmas display. How exciting. We need more than that. If not for us, then for all the kids. Folks are starting to move back into Detroit. They now have a big tree and a skating rink downtown. More and more holiday decorations are going up along with holiday markets. Perhaps Dan Gilbert will put a big Christmas display in the new building he's building on the old Hudson's site. I hope so. Metro Detroit is too big, too important, and too cold in winter to not have some magic at Christmas.

# NATIONAL POLISH AMERICAN
# SPORTS HALL OF FAME

CHICAGO IS THE NUMBER ONE American city for Polish Catholics. Chicago has the Polish American Museum and the International Polka Association. One thing Chicago doesn't have is the Polish American Sports Hall of Fame. That's right here in the Motor City. Well, actually it's in Troy, but close enough.

Few nationalities love or play sports more than the Polish. Not just bowling, like the comedians say, but all sports. In 1973, a group of Polish Detroiters got together and decided to form an organization that would recognize our great athletes. They formed the National Polish American Sports Hall of Fame.

Since 1973, the NPASHF has awarded 128 athletes in twenty-one different sports. To be nominated, your father or mother must be Polish. The awards are given at a banquet held every June at the Polish American Cultural Center in Troy. There, they place a plaque on the wall in their honor. The plaques are hanging all over the place. Also, lining the walls are display cabinets with different sports memorabilia that winners have donated over the years. It's worth a trip just to see this amazing stuff. Also while your there you can get a great Polish dinner at the Wawel restaurant.

I get excited every time I go there and walk around reading all the plaques. There are Polish greats in every sport: Mike Ditka for football, Pete Stemkowski for hockey, Mike Krzyzewski (Coach K) for basketball, Killer Kowalski for wrestling, and of course, Ed Lubanski for bowling, to mention a few.

The very first award given by the NPASHF was given to a Polish boy from Donora, Pennsylvania, named Stan Musial. Stan "The Man" Musial was one of America's greatest players in America's greatest sport—baseball. Stan played first base and outfield for the St. Louis Cardinals. He played in twenty-four All-Star Games and in three World Series. He had a lifetime batting average of 331. He had 3,630 hits which included 475 home runs. Bleacher Report picked Stan as the eleventh greatest baseball player of all time. I think it should be higher, but it is still ahead of many greats including Joe DiMaggio and Mickey Mantle. Stan also helped start a college scholarship fund for the NPASHF, which is awarded to Polish American High School athletes every year at the banquet.

The NPASHF has a sports panel board that vote for the nominees. I just so happen to be on that board. The reason I got on the board is a funny story. A person who was on the voting board, also named Robert Dombrowski, died. My friend, Buck Jerzy, nominated me to replace him. "They won't even have to change the name on the stationary," he told them. It worked, and I got on. I don't get nominated to very many boards.

The Robert Dombrowski that I replaced is a person I should note. He was wealthy. I heard that he had something to do with inventing the fax machine, but I don't really know if that's true. But what I do know to be true is he donated money to Orchard Lake St. Mary's to build their athletic field house, which they named the Robert Dombrowski Fieldhouse. Great name!

Orchard Lake Saint Mary's is a school and seminary with big Polish roots. Located twenty-five miles northwest of Detroit, it sits on 125 beautiful acres right on Orchard Lake. They got their start over a hundred years ago on the lower east side of Detroit.

In the late 1800s, Detroit's very first Polish parish, Saint Albertus, got a new priest from Wisconsin named Father Jozef Dabroski.

Father Dabroski recognized the need for a seminary for Polish-American priests. In 1885, Father Dabroski opened the SS Cyril and Methodius Seminary on St. Aubin Street in Detroit. Father Dabroski also is credited with introducing the Felician Sisters to America.

A few years later, the Michigan Military Academy that was originally on the Orchard Lake site closed and sold the seminary their property. In 1909, the SS Cyril and Methodius Seminary moved from Detroit to its new home on Orchard Lake. Later, they opened a small college and high school on the site naming both St. Mary's.

Today Orchard Lake St. Mary's, as the high school is called, is the most famous of the three institutions. The high school, like most Catholic all-boys high schools, have become an athletic powerhouse. Their football team, called the Eaglets, has amassed a .709 winning percentage since 1956.

Orchard Lake still maintains its Polish tradition. Pope John Paul II stayed on campus when he was younger. They have the Polish Home Army museum at Orchard Lake. And every year, Orchard Lake St. Mary's has a great big Polish festival with rides and games and beer tents and, of course, pierogies!

I have to mention Buck Jerzy, the person who got me on the NPASHF sports panel board. Buck is a former sports writer and football statistician for Notre Dame University. He was commodore and perhaps last remaining member of the Downtown Boat Club and a tricky card player. Born and raised in Hamtramck, Buck gets my vote for the Duke of Polish Detroiters. Buck seems to know everyone, and everyone knows Buck. I think if Buck had accompanied us when we saw Pope John Paul, the pope would have stopped and turned and said, "Buck, is that you?"

# Trip to Poland

AFTER ALL THESE YEARS, MY wife and I finally took a trip to Poland. What a trip it was. We flew from Budapest to Warsaw. The Warsaw airport was very clean and unobtrusive for a European capital city airport. While waiting for my bags at the conveyer belt, I noticed signs written in English warning people to watch out for crooked taxi drivers. As I read the sign, I could see my wife negotiating with a taxi driver who already had her suitcase firmly in his grip. The three of us just walked out the airport to his ratty minivan. Unexpectedly, there wasn't an immigration check. The taxi driver wasn't too bad. He only charged us twice what the ride should have cost, but he got us to the hotel safe and sound. Welcome to Poland.

Waiting for us at the hotel was our tour guide, Sasha, a young blond Polish girl who spoke excellent English. She told us that all young people in Poland are taught English in school as a second language as opposed to the older Poles who were taught Russian. Times change. "Bags in the hallway at 6:30 a.m., and the bus leaves at eight sharp!" she said. *Oh Lord*, I thought. *This isn't going to be a rest trip.* Sasha then said, "If you need anything, there is a mall right across the street."

It didn't look like a mall from the outside. It was an old brick building on a narrow city street, but when we opened the door and went inside, wow! It was a huge modern mall with five floors top to bottom. Snazzy-looking shoppers were everywhere and shopping the same stores found in all the upscale American malls. Forget about the old stories of stuffing suitcases with Levi jeans to sell in Europe.

There was Levi, Old Navy, Nike, and just about any other brand I could think of right in the heart of Warsaw.

As a kid growing up, my parents would tell me sad stories of people in Poland waiting in bread lines. I don't know if that was true, but there weren't any bread lines now. The only line I saw was at McDonald's, and it was probably tourists.

The next morning at eight sharp, we were in the tour bus rolling through downtown Warsaw, the new section. There were modern tall buildings with familiar names scrolled across their tops: Google, IBM, and Mercedes-Benz. Warsaw, like most of Poland, is a tale of two worlds: the old and new.

The old town goes back to the thirteenth century with very old buildings in pristine condition. It is hard to imagine that the Germans in World War II destroyed this entire town. After they destroyed it, the Polish people piled all the bricks and pieces of each building on its same property and then using the old bricks, rebuilt the buildings exactly as they were.

Every Polish city has a mythical symbol. Warsaw's symbol is a mermaid holding a sword and shield named Syrena. Legend has it that a fisherman named Wars was fishing in the Vistula river, and a mermaid swam up and told him to build a city on the banks of the river. He did, and to name it, he combined his name, Wars, and his wife's name, Sawa, to make the name Warsaw.

The Warsaw mermaid, Syrena, can be seen everywhere: on trains, buses, taxis, and statues. The main Syrena statue is right next to the Vistula River and is an actual symbol of a true hero. The model that posed for the statue was a twenty-three-year-old student named Krystyna Krahelska. During World War II, she became a member of the Polish Underground Army and was killed on the first day of the Warsaw Uprising. Amazing!

Warsaw is a great city on par with all the great cities of Europe. The city is filled with parks, cathedrals, palaces, monuments, and museums. The tallest building in Warsaw (767 feet) is called the Palace of Culture and Science. It was built in 1953, a gift from Joseph Stalin and the Soviet Union. In front of the US Embassy is a statue of Ronald Regan. "Tear down that wall!"

The next city on our tour was Gdańsk, and I couldn't have been more excited. It seems everyone who goes to Poland loves Gdańsk. It is a medieval city of canals. It looks a lot like Amsterdam. Gdańsk sits right on the Baltic and is known as the Amber capital of the world. The mythical symbol of Gdańsk is Neptune, the god of the sea. In the heart of Gdańsk is St. Mary's church, the biggest brick gothic church in the world.

We went to the Gdańsk shipyards where Solidarity first started and ultimately brought down the Soviet Union and communism. The front area is called Solidarity Square. They have a large building called the European Solidarity Centre built out of rusty steel to represent a ship's hull. Next to that, they have three tall crosses with a sea anchor attached to each one. The entrance gate to the shipyard is decorated with fresh-cut flowers and pictures of Pope John Paul.

We then walked along the canals and stopped at the Gdańsk Crane. It was the biggest port crane in medieval Europe back when Gdańsk was one of the largest shipping centers in the world. The old buildings now are touristy with the usual things like bars and coffee shops. They also had a bakery that made paczki, and they were delicious!

Malbork Castle is the biggest fortress in Europe and probably the world. It sits on the Nogat River. Driving up to the castle, I was surprised that it sat alone with nothing around it, just a huge brick fortress that is fifty-two acres in size. After all, it has been here for eight hundred years. Wouldn't people want to live close just for protection? Or wouldn't some builder want to build a bunch of houses nearby and call it Malbork Acres?

Malbork Castle was the home of the Teutonic Knights; those brave warriors who fought in the Crusades. Unfortunately, they lost Israel to the Muslims. Nobody wins them all. During World War II, after Germany took over Poland, the Germans used this fortress as a camp for the Hitler Youth.

It had indoor facilities that were interesting and rare I think for the thirteenth century. The bathroom had wooden seats with a round hole where the waste would just drop down to the floor below.

What happened to the waste then, I don't know, perhaps a job for the Hitler Youth.

The next town we came to was Torun, which sits on the Vistula River. Torun is the home of Copernicus, the world's greatest astronomer. Torun's mythical symbol is a frog. Torun is a lovely little European city with narrow pristine streets lined with attractive shops. Torun is a UNESCO-designated site as were many of the places we visited in Poland. There are fourteen UNESCO sites in Poland. The USA has twenty-three.

About this time, I started getting sick. I was that guy on the bus coughing, sneezing, and hacking things up. You know, the one everyone tries to get away from. Sasha came up and asked if I wanted to see a doctor. "Yes," I told her. Besides, I wanted to learn about the Polish health-care system.

That night after dinner, she came to our room with a doctor. He checked me out. *Pretty well*, I thought. He informed me in broken English that I had a bad cold and charged me the equivalent of $95 dollars US. Then he drove Sasha and me to an all-night pharmacy where they filled four prescriptions for me for around $20 dollars US. A total of $115. *Not bad*, I thought, *for a house call, ride to the pharmacy, and four prescriptions*. Sasha then handed me a form she had written up with all the charges on it. "Save this form, and when you get home, you can turn it in to your health insurance company and get all your money back," she said. I don't think she understands the American health-care system.

Czestochowa is the town that people go to see the famous Black Madonna painting. It is the iconic picture of Mary holding the baby Jesus, both with dark faces. It is the same picture that hangs on the wall of most Polish homes in America, including ours. This painting is one of the national symbols of Poland. They say you cannot visit Poland without going to Czestochowa and see the Black Madonna. It is the third most visited Christian shrine in the world.

The painting is located in a monastery that became a fortress called Jasna Góra. It is built on top of a hill and has a huge tower (106 meters); the tallest in Poland that overlooks the city. Thousands of tourists come to Czestochowa every day to see the Black Madonna. It's amazing. Every group gets a priest to guide you in.

Our priest / tour guide was pretty humorous. When he found out we were from Detroit, he got excited and shouted out, "Orchard Lake St. Mary's!"

"Yep, it's still there," I told him. He was a joke teller. "How do you make holy water? You boil the hell out of it!"

As we got closer, the jokes stopped, and we all became silent. We were getting closer to the place where the Black Madonna hung. The painting sits on top of a magnificent altar in a gorgeous baroque-styled chapel. A service was going on, but we were still allowed to walk right up to the altar to get a close look. It gave me goosebumps. I could see the sword cuts put on the painting by the Mongols in the thirteenth century. They say Saint Luke the Evangelist painted the painting from life on cypress wood pieces from Mary's own table. The painting darkened from a fire set by the attacking Swedish in 1655. The monks held them off for forty days, then on Christmas Eve, the Swedes left. It was a great victory for the outnumbered Polish.

That night, we went to an old Polish inn to eat, drink, and watch traditional Polish dancers. When we walked in, we had to drink a glass of vodka the Polish way: by locking arms and downing it straight without a chaser. Everybody drank vodka, and everybody took turns Polish dancing. It was lots of fun.

On the bus ride back, Sasha put a disk in of American music, as she called it, and turned it up loud! The Polish call all rock-type popular music American music! Later in a conversation, my wife, Linda, made the comment, "Well, you know everyone hates us, Americans." Something that just about every American has said or thought at one time or another.

"What are you talking about?" Sasha said. "Americans are the most loved people on the planet. Everybody loves Americans." Yep, that's how most Polish people think.

Krakow is the Ann Arbor or Cambridge of Poland. It is a very old beautiful college town, home to the world-famous Jagiellonian University. Many say that Krakow is the most beautiful city in Poland. I can't argue with that. Krakow was the only Polish city to come through World War II essentially undamaged. Krakow was the capital of Poland from the eleventh century until the sixteenth century. It has the Wawel Castle; the place where the kings lived back in the Middle Ages when Poland was a superpower.

In the heart of the city is Market Square. It was built in the fourteenth century. It was the largest square in medieval Europe. Right next to Market Square is St. Mary's Church where at the top of every hour, a Krakow fireman plays the bugle from the church tower, warning the town that the Tatar's were invading, which happened in 1241. The fireman stops on the exact note the original bugler stopped on when he was shot and killed by a Tatar arrow so many years ago.

It was a beautiful day, and my wife and I luckily found a table in the square and ordered lunch. Polish food in Poland is different than the food in Polish restaurants back home. Pork roast and turkey, lots of vegetables, soup, and pierogis, always pierogis. We hardly saw any kielbasa, kapusta, or golompkies, which are Polish staples back home. Most Polish meals are basic old-school-styled meals along with pierogies and delicious deserts. The Polish eat this way for lunch and dinner. Rarely did I see them eating junk food including the young. And most of them are pretty skinny.

As Linda and I were sitting at our table in the square enjoying some delicious beet soup, a young Polish girl with a great big smile asked if she could join us. It turns out she was a lawyer (Yes, they have them in Poland.) who, like most Polish people, loves America and Americans. She told us that she's been to America a couple of times usually to New York where she has friends and family.

While we sat and chatted, a group of peaceful protesters walked by carrying signs protesting Fascism. Krakow is a college town with college kids doing what college kids do. I asked her if she was afraid of being attacked again since Poland is right on the Russian border.

"No, of course not. Why should we?" she laughingly said.

Every Polish person that I asked that question to, gave the same response. They seem to have no fear of Russia or anybody else. What a brave race of people. Especially after all that have they been through.

Then she told us a story of the last time that she was in America and tried to visit Canada. She was stopped at the border. "It was horrible. They took me in a room and strip-searched me. Then the guards questioned me for hours. It reminded me of the old Soviet Union!"

It is alarming to hear something like this, especially in Europe, where going from one country to another is just like going from Michigan to Ohio. Entering Poland, and most other European countries, there are no border guards, no checkpoints, just a sign reading "Welcome to Poland."

The Wieliczka salt mines are another must-see stop in Poland. They are gigantic mines over one thousand feet deep. It is the only salt mine in the world where mining has continued since the middle ages. They have mined salt here from 1300 right up until 2007. But people don't come here just to see an old mine. They come here to see the amazing things the Polish miners have done to this place.

They built a huge ballroom and a church made entirely out of salt, chandeliers and all. They also have built a mining museum showing you how it was mining salt in the middle ages. The miners built everything on their own time after working all day in the mines. Their dedicated hard work will last forever as an amazing legacy.

"*Work will set you free!*" says the overhead sign as you walk into Auschwitz. It is written in German and placed there in the 1940s by the Germans. But work did not set you free, especially in Auschwitz.

Auschwitz and its neighbor, Birkenau, even after all these years, are the most horrible memorials on Earth. It was the devil's workshop if there is a devil or a god. And after seeing this place in person, you must wonder. One-and-a-half million people were put to death here: young people, old people, and little children, doing nothing wrong, just for being people that the Nazis didn't like. Madness!

Auschwitz was originally a Polish Army base. It was abandoned by 1939 when the Germans invaded Poland. The Germans reopened it at first as a prisoner-of-war camp, then after a while, they started bringing in the Jews and other undesirables: gypsies, homosexuals, and Polish Catholics to name a few. By war's end, the Germans killed

1.5 million people in Auschwitz of which 150,000 or 10 percent were Polish Catholic.

The numbers don't tell the whole story. I heard these numbers all my life, but it never hit me until I actually walked through the place and actually looked at the gas chambers and the crematoriums firsthand. They have methodically maintained both camps, and the Polish tour guides are very good. The tours are in English with nothing held back. Piles of the poor victim's suitcases, clothes, and shoes are still there. The pile of little children's shoes was the hardest to look at.

They explained to us that the smartest minds of Germany designed these death camps. Thousands of Germans were brought in to work here. All the Polish people living in the surrounding communities were moved out, and their houses were given to the German workers and their families. The smell of burning bodies could be smelled for miles. After the war, the German population claimed they had no knowledge of these death camps but that can't be true as we learned.

Auschwitz was the devil's workshop; a shrine to man's hatred of man pristinely preserved. Every American who comes here and sees it firsthand will be moved. I promise.

Of course, there was a lot more to this trip than written on these pages. Poland is a peaceful place filled with beautiful, charming, and intelligent people. It has low crime rate, clean streets, nice people, and cool cities. I sure wouldn't mind living there.

# FUNKY COLD CZARNINA

NOPE, THIS IS NOT THE recipe for duck's blood soup that nobody eats. It's just a couple of unique stories that a book about the Polish in Michigan should not leave out.

The first is the *Polish Muslims*, a hilarious rock group from Hamtramck and the eastern side of Detroit. The band members are not Muslim at all. They are Polish Catholics. They sometimes even pass out rosaries at their concerts. I got one. But the name is comical.

The Polish Muslims started thirty-seven years ago in 1981. Back then, Detroit had these black groups that just the name would scare the crap out of us whites: The Black Panthers and The Black Muslims. So when the fun name Polish Muslims came out, we couldn't stop laughing, and the laughing continued right through the concert.

They take songs we know by heart and switch them around into funny Polish refrains such as The Beach Boys "Surfing USA" becomes "Bowling USA." Hey, Detroit doesn't have a surfing ocean, but we do have a bunch of bowling alleys. "Love Potion No. 9" becomes "Love Polka No. 9," and The Beatles's "Yesterday" becomes "Paczki Day," the song for this book when it becomes a movie.

No Polish fair in the Detroit area is complete without the Muslims; just having them doubles the attendance. A band for the whole family everyone from dziecko's to busha's. Their shows are big fun with everyone on his or her feet dancing the polka and singing, "Strike, strike. Spare, spare. Bowling USA!"

The second story is about a Polish restaurant located three hundred miles north of Detroit called *Legs Inn*. Legs Inn is in Cross Village on the road M119 also called *The Tunnel of Trees*; one of the most scenic drives in the whole state. The restaurant is built entirely from wood logs, a work of art that the creator, Stanley Smolak, built over ninety years ago.

Stanley Smolak immigrated from Kamionka, Poland, to the USA in 1912. He left what was then occupied Poland to avoid being drafted into the Austrian Army. Like many Polish refuges, he got a job in Detroit working in the auto plant. He worked hard and saved his zlotys, then in 1921, he moved to Cross Village to build his dream.

Stanley bought a beautiful piece of land and chopped down the trees and dug up the stones that he used to build his inn. Everything in Legs Inn is built by Stanley and built by hand. The walls, the ceiling, the tables, the chairs, everything is built from wood. Stanley is also an artist, and it shows in his work. There are totem poles and other artifacts that Stanley built to pay tribute to Native Americans, the only other people who lived around there back then.

Today Legs Inn is a popular tourist destination that folks often wait in line to eat there. Everything is painstakingly preserved; all the beautiful furniture and carvings Stanley made over the years. They have three-stone fireplaces and a lovely garden overlooking Lake Michigan. Stanley is gone, but the Smolak family still own and run the business and they keep it just as it was.

They have great Polish food; everything from pierogi to bigos. They even have these little kielbasa that they call kabanosy. Delicious. And all your favorite Polish beers right in the heart of Northern Michigan.

Last time we were there, we had a young Polish college student named Ada who waited on us. She told us this was her third summer working there. I asked her how she liked America. She looked around and said, "Here, I feel like I'm still in Poland."

Legs Inn has entertainment on some evenings. I wonder if they ever had the Polish Muslims. Now that would make a fun trip up north.

# WINNERS WRITE THE HISTORY

POLAND IS A COUNTRY WITH a thousand-year history. It is a land that has given the world much. It is a land that stepped up to defend its friends even though their friends have often failed to defend them. It is a land that once was a European power and then was completely removed from the map.

After 130 years of nonexistence, Poland got their country back in 1920 only to be taken twenty years later by the Germans and then the Russians. For fifty years, they were controlled by Russia, and the world stood by and did nothing.

Detroit was a city that people came to from all over the world to build a better life for themselves, and they were warmly welcomed. They got good jobs and built houses on beautiful tree-lined streets. They sent their kids to great schools, lived in crime-free neighborhoods, and enjoyed one of the highest standards of living in America. They came from everywhere: Ireland, Italy, the Middle East, but of the many people that moved here and appreciated this city, the most were from Poland.

Then the factories started to move out and the people started to move out, and before we knew it, Detroit looked like a ghost town. It became a national joke. Another joke, I guess, to go along with all the Polish jokes. Detroit finally went bankrupt, and just like Poland, nobody came to help.

Poland kicked the Russians out, rebuilt their country, and changed their government. Today Poland is a land every Polish person in the world can be proud of. It is a modern, beautiful, and prosperous country. Poland today is the land of the free and the home of the brave. Poland, I think, has that same spirit America must have had in 1776.

Detroit today is becoming one of America's great success stories, thanks to Detroiters who stepped up and brought the city back. They got a new mayor, a new government, and began to rebuild the city. New buildings, refurbished buildings, and young folks can be seen everywhere. Thousands of millennials have moved from their parent's suburban neighborhoods to live and work in Detroit. Maybe they're looking for the life their parents had when they lived in the city.

Detroit was a great place to live. Ask anyone who grew up there in the forties, fifties, and sixties; they will all agree. I have never met a Polish person who wasn't proud of their nationality. Despite the stupid jokes and adages that we had to endure, we love being Polish. Nothing comes easy, and there have been some tough times, but we overcame the tough times. We are tough people. And in the end, when our history is written, it will be written by us because we are winners. I hope this book will help.

# DOMBROWSKI
# FAMILY RECIPES

# Bobs Kapusta

1 c. elbow macaroni  
32 oz. bag of sauerkraut  
1 medium onion, diced  
1/4 lb. bacon, diced  

1 Tbsp. caraway seed  
3 Tbsp. brown sugar  
1/4 tsp. pepper  

Boil and drain the macaroni as directed and set aside.

Fry the bacon over medium heat for five minutes, then add the onion and fry another five minutes.

Rinse the sauerkraut, then put the sauerkraut and macaroni into a roasting pan.

Add the onion bacon mix, then sprinkle the caraway seed, brown sugar, and pepper.

Mix everything, then cover and bake at 325 degrees for one hour.

# Lillian's Cookie Sheet Apple Pie

## Crust

3 c. flour                      1/2 tsp. salt
1 1/2 sticks butter or shortening    1 c. ice water

In a large bowl add the flour, butter, and salt.

Using two forks, cut the butter into the flour until butter is small crumbled pieces.

Slowly add the water while tossing mix with a fork until crust doesn't stick to the sides of the bowl.

Form crust into a ball and place in refrigerator for one hour.

## Filling

10 apples, peeled and diced      1/2 tsp. salt
2 c. sugar                     3 Tbsp. butter
1 Tbsp. cinnamon

Mix all ingredients in bowl and set aside.

## Pie

Cut flour in two; roll larger half on floured board and place in 10" by 15" cookie sheet. Add filling and dot with butter. Cover with top crust and make a few slits. Brush pie top lightly with milk and lightly sprinkle with sugar. Bake at 450 degrees for fifteen minutes, then at 350 degrees for fifty minutes. Enjoy.

# HENRIETTA'S POLISH CHEESE CAKE

| | |
|---|---|
| 2 lbs. farmer's cheese | 4 eggs separated |
| 3 Tbsp. flour | 3/4 cup sweetened condensed |
| 2 tsp. vanilla | milk |
| 1 box graham cracker crumbs | 3 sticks butter, melted |
| 3 c. sugar | |

Beat egg whites for ten minutes or until stiff, then refrigerate. Mix melted butter and graham cracker crumbs and form into crust in a 9" by 13" baking pan. Mix cheese, flour, egg yolks, and vanilla. Gently fold in egg whites (do not mix). Pour into crust and sprinkle remaining graham cracker crumbs on top. Bake at 350 degrees for forty-five minutes to one hour.

# GOLABKI (STUFFED CABBAGE)

1 large head cabbage
1 large onion, diced
1 lb. ground beef
1 lb. ground pork
2 c. cooked rice

1 tsp. salt
1/2 tsp. pepper
2 cans Campbell's tomato soup
2 cups of water
1/2 tsp. garlic powder

Shove a large fork into the core of the cabbage. Carefully lift and place into a large kettle of boiling water. Using a sharp knife while holding the fork, cut around the core slowly freeing the cabbage leaves. As the leaves float up, remove the leaves with tongs until you have twenty-five or thirty. Trim the center stem from each leaf. Chop up the remaining cabbage.

Mix the onion, ground beef, ground pork, rice, garlic, salt, and pepper.

Place one heaping tablespoon of mix in a cabbage leaf, tuck sides over filling, then roll tight. Repeat until cabbage leaves and mix is used up.

Place half of the chopped cabbage in a large roasting pan, fill with layers of cabbage rolls, stem side down, then cover with remaining chopped cabbage.

Mix the soup and water and pour over cabbage rolls, lightly salt, and pepper.

Cover and bake at 325 degrees until beef and pork are cooked about ninety minutes.

# Bigos (Polish Stew)
## *The National Dish of Poland*

2 Tbsp. olive oil
1 lb. pork, diced
1 lb. kielbasa, sliced
4 slices bacon, diced
1 large onion, diced
2 carrots, sliced
1 lb. mushrooms, sliced
3 cloves garlic, chopped
1/2 head cabbage, shredded
32 oz. bag of sauerkraut, rinsed
1 c. dry red wine

1 1/4 oz. can diced tomatoes
4 cups beef broth
1 bay leaf
1/2 tsp. thyme
1 tsp. all spice
2 Tbsp. paprika
1 tsp. caraway seed
1 tsp. salt
1/2 tsp. pepper
1 c. pitted prunes, chopped

In a large stew pot, heat olive oil over medium heat.

Add bacon and onions and sauté for three minutes.

Add pork and kielbasa and sauté for five minutes.

Add all the rest of the ingredients except the prunes.

Raise the heat high while watching and stirring until stew bubbles.

Turn heat to low, partially cover, and cook for three hours while stirring every fifteen minutes.

Remove bay leaf and add prunes; cook for ten more minutes.

# PIEROGI

2 1/2 c. flour                    1/2 tsp. salt
2 eggs beaten                    1/2 c. warm water

Mix flour and salt in bowl; make a well in the center and add eggs.

With your hands, mix the eggs into the flour while slowly adding the water.

Knead dough with your hands; sprinkle a little more flour over dough if needed.

Form dough into a ball and refrigerate for a half hour.

# Cheese Filling

2 c. farmer's cheese
1 Tbsp. sugar
1/4 tsp. salt
1 egg

# Potato Filling

2 c. mashed potatoes
4 Tbsp. sour cream
1/4 tsp. salt
1/4 tsp. pepper

# SAUERKRAUT FILLING

2 c. sauerkraut
1/2 medium onion diced and lightly sautéed
1/4 tsp. salt
1/4 tsp. pepper

Cut dough in half and roll out on a floured board like pie dough.
Using a glass or cookie cutter, cut out three-inch rounds.
Place a spoonful of filling in each round and fold over.
Moisten edges and firmly press edges together.
Drop pierogi into boiling water for three to five minutes until
they float. Remove with a slotted spoon and lightly fry in butter.

# KOLACKY (POLISH COOKIES) A CHRISTMAS FAVORITE

12 oz. butter, softened
8 oz. cream cheese
2 c. flour

1 Tbsp. sugar
2 c. jam
1/2 c. powder sugar for dusting

Cream butter, cream cheese, and sugar, then slowly add the flour. Dough will be sticky.

Divide dough into two balls and wrap each in plastic wrap then chill for one hour.

Roll out dough on a floured board. Using a pizza cutter, cut into two- or three-inch squares.

Place 1 teaspoon of jam in center and fold over the corners and press together. Moisten corners with egg white to help stick.

Bake at 375 degrees for ten to eleven minutes on an ungreased cookie sheet.

Remove from sheet and dust with powder sugar.

# PACZKI

*If you don't live by a Polish bakery, then make your own Paczki by following this simple recipe.*

| | |
|---|---|
| 12 egg yolks | 1/2 c. sugar |
| 2 packs of active dry yeast | 4 c. flour |
| 1 tsp. salt | 1 c. heavy cream hot |
| 1/4 c. warm water | 2–8 oz. jars of fruit preserves |
| 1/2 c. softened butter | |

Oil for frying.

Soften yeast in warm water.

Beat egg yolks and salt in mixer.

Beat butter and sugar; mix well and add yeast.

Stir in half of flour and half of cream into yeast mix, then add other half; mix well and add egg mix; beat for two minutes.

Cover bowl with plastic, let rise, then punch down; do this twice.

Roll dough on a floured surface to 3/4" thick.

Cut out 3" rounds.

Cover doughnuts and let rise until doubled about twenty minutes.

Fry doughnuts in hot oil until golden brown on each side.

Remove and drain on paper towel and sprinkle with sugar.

When cooled, cut small hole in the side of each doughnut.

Using a pastry filler, squeeze about a tablespoon of jam into each doughnut.

# About the Author

BOB DOMBROWSKI WAS BORN AND raised in the city of Detroit.

He worked for thirty-eight years as a Detroit firefighter and managed to survive that and Detroit's bankruptcy (so far). He has been happily married to his wife, Linda, for forty years. They have three sons and four grandchildren. Besides writing, Bob likes to spend his time reading, cooking, music, watching old movies, cheering Detroit sports teams, riding his bike, going to the Y, walking his dog, and socializing with friends and family while always saving time for evening cocktails.

Bob and Linda split their time between their home in Michigan and a second home in Sarasota, Florida.

9 781645 440628